Exciting Moments
versus Boring routine

Exciting ideas for turning routine and
boredom into more joy of living

THEO KERSTJENS

authorHOUSE®

AuthorHouse™ UK Ltd.
500 Avebury Boulevard
Central Milton Keynes, MK9 2BE
www.authorhouse.co.uk
Phone: 08001974150

First published by AuthorHouse 3/3/2010

ISBN: 978-1-4490-8837-8 (sc)

This book is printed on acid-free paper.

Contents

PART II: "THE MIND IN THE SETTING"

PART III: KEEP THE MIND EXCITED!

Preface

Why does anyone sit down and write a book? What gave me the inspiration to write this book in particular? It's quite simple. I've had the privilege to travel over four million miles, boarding countless planes and touching down in scores of destinations throughout the world. This has given me the tremendous opportunity to learn about many different races and cultures and have exiting encounters with thousands of unique individuals. As a communications professional, an important part of my job is to observe and get to know each new place and its people in depth. I've dedicated years of my life to listening to people's words and thoughts, conversing with them about trivial daily matters and what mattered most to them, and observing what they do and why and how they do it. In summary, my life has always been the polar opposite of routine and boredom.

The more I became aware of just how privileged I was to travel and be constantly stimulated by the world around me, the more I realized that many people I met did not have the daily opportunity to be inspired by a pulse of new sensations– the stimulation necessary to conquer what is certainly one of the most deadly agents out to kill our joy of living: THE ROUTINE. I have witnessed the deadly effect of the "routine virus" on people's inspiration and aspirations. I have often seen sadness and boredom in the eyes of those who welcomed me and felt the lack of energy in their otherwise friendly handshakes. The more I used my wonderful free time during flights between destinations to read, reflect, and write about why some people's lives are exciting and fulfilling and others' are not, the more it became clear to me that no one is immune to the routine virus and that we all must actively protect ourselves from its harmful effects.

Spiritually deadening routine has become endemic in all cultures and spheres of life, although some show signs of being are more resistant than others. It affects people regardless of their gender, social status, or profession. The virus enters living rooms, kitchens, bedrooms, schools, and the work place, indiscriminately attacking all the vital and healthy relationships in its path. There is almost no place where it does not rear its ugly head and destroy the inspiration and the aspirations of the people it infects.

These are enough reasons to seek ways to rise above the current wave of negative thinking and use our mind power to break the routine and discover how to add more excitement and joy to our lives.

This book is not intended to substitute professional treatment in dealing with serious advanced depressions. *It is a guide that gives healthy minds easy, practical, and creative suggestions for forging a new positive mindset that can transform usual boring situations into extraordinary experiences.* It is meant to inspire its readers to spread their wings and discover a whole new range of possibilities for living life to the fullest.

Let's spread the wings of our mind and take off together. Flying over new landscapes, we will learn how each of us can have a superb birds-eye view of the amazing world we live in and discover our many hidden talents. With a bit of courage and some landing practice, we will explore together the many ways that we can beat the routine and live happier lives.

If this book can make only a small contribution toward other people's happiness it will have been worth the effort. We only live once, and we all deserve to experience many moments of inspiration and nurture the higher aspirations that will make us feel happy to be alive instead of feeling bored to death. Once we establish a harmonious balance between our inner needs and desires and our worldly responsibilities, we will feel immune to the routine virus and be empowered and inspired to share more exciting moments with those we love.

Let's give NEW WINGS to our lives!

Theo Kerstjens Flight: TK Wings 2010

Acknowledgements

This book is dedicated to the thousands of everyday people from different cultures and diverse socio-economic backgrounds whom I have met around the world:

Special thanks are due to those individuals who have demonstrated the art of bringing excitement into their lives and the lives of others.

Not less important have been the people who have sincerely confided to me that their lives were far from exciting: warm-hearted people who struggled in cold, unfeeling environments and others who, despite of the warmth that surrounded them, remained discontented and unfulfilled. Together, they inspired me to observe and to analyze human nature from a different point of view. These people proved to me that excitement and fulfillment are not given things in everyone's lives, but are essential elements of our health and happiness that must be sincerely desired and actively pursued every day.

This book owes much to experts whose research findings gave me useful insights into the amazing and complex functions of our mind at both the conscious and unconscious levels.

Credit must also be given to those who trusted in my skills as a communicator and gave me the opportunity to travel and work in many places across the globe, enjoying my job while providing for my family. They too, have indirectly contributed to this book.

I am especially indebted to my beloved wife and children, who too often did without my daily presence and support. They have always kept me motivated on the road, particularly in those moments when their absence made me aware that in spite of the warmth of those we meet around the world, home really is "sweet home".

I would especially like to recognize my wife's creative talent, good taste, and unique ideas that have added so much to our multi-faceted life together over the years. She has always been an unfailing source of inspiration for creating endless "exciting moments".

PART 1 THE MINDSET

How is everything today? As usual, Thank-you!

Who hasn't heard or uttered these platitudes millions of times? In a broader sense, saying that everything is **"as usual!"** is an admission that nothing special is happening; that one is stuck in a rather boring daily routine. Approaching it from a different angle, it can be diagnosed as the **ROUTINE virus**! Of course, positive routines do exist and people who are naturally extremely organized and work in professions that require repetition might thrive on a daily diet of routines. But this book is not about positive routines; it is about energy-draining and de-motivating ones and the highly contagious **"as usual"** mentality that threatens to kill our inspiration and take the fun and excitement out of our lives. Let's start with some deeper reflections about the banalities repeated every second by millions of people around the world: words and actions that at first glance seem so innocuous. Close your eyes for just one minute and imagine you are listening to the phrase **"as usual!"** repeated over and over again in the same monotone voice – forty times in the space of one minute. If you do this, you may come to the conclusion: "How boring! It almost makes me sick!"

That's exactly what it can do, make you sick. Imagine eating tomato soup, beans and rice, or bread with peanut butter forty consecutive times without a break; or listening to the same song, lesson, criticism, or even the same compliment, forty times. Imagine embracing your lover in exactly the

1

same way forty times, watching the same television program forty times, producing the same product or performing the same service forty times, walking forty times down the same road or wearing the same dress forty times, etc. Enough with the forty times! Stop the boring repetition! "Yes!" I hear your inner voice saying, "but that's what life is often about: the same, more of the same, or the very, very similar!" It's true that social structures and mechanisms, belief systems, and ingrained behavior patterns have us in their grip and even lay traps for us, often making it difficult to escape from "as usual" situations and habits. But it is also true that not everything in our life has to be always as usual as we might tend to believe. As long as we can regularly escape from some of the usual, we can steer ourselves away from the rut of the routine and put ourselves firmly on the road toward the changes, challenges, and inspirations that will lead us to interesting places and opportunities for unusual and exciting experiences. If we do otherwise, the result is clear: Everything goes on as usual. There is little or no excitement, little or no joy of living.

> **"The two enemies of human happiness are pain and boredom."** –Arthur Schopenhauer

How "As usual" thinking can create a cascade of de-motivation and "de-inspiration"

When they wake up in the morning, millions of people have trouble dragging themselves out of bed because they dread confronting yet another day of routine with no emotional reward. They feel like robots and may, in fact, be holding down jobs that a robot or a computer program could do just as well. Perhaps their working environment isn't very inspirational either, and they don't receive the financial remuneration or the recognition they think they deserve. Maybe they even feel undervalued, and are weighed down by the general sense of indifference that surrounds them. The same daily rituals await them: the lackluster greetings of others sharing the same typical morning mood or the same toast and coffee shared in a silence that amplifies the sound of the rain pouring down outside. This is not a very encouraging scenario, but of course, things can get worse when they walk out of the door a few minutes later. The usual morning stress of getting the kids off to school and the inevitable, unnerving effect of rush hour traffic is reflected in the bored and yawning faces in the other cars stopping for a red light. When they reach work, they exchange the same programmed good morning greetings that perfectly confirm the general mood: **"How is everything today?"** is met with the pre programmed answer: **"As Usual!"**

With this kind of start, what can we expect the rest of day is going to be like? What can we expect if most of the days of the week, the month, and the year follow the same pattern? Obviously a boring year and a boring life, although the evening could still make up for the disappointing daytime hours. Let's imagine someone called John arriving home in the afternoon from work:

> John pulls up in front of his home. He doesn't line the car up perfectly with the curb because he has no intention of leaving it parked for the night just yet. He wants to pick up Mary and take her for a relaxing walk in the country. As usual, Mary has forgotten to close the garage door. Looking in, John sees her car, and next to it, a picnic basket. As always, she must have already prepared their favorite snacks for their after-work afternoon escape. The window of the upper bedroom opens and Mary pops her head out, throwing him kiss. "Here I am, honey. I'll be down in a flash," she calls out. John returns the long-distance kiss and pulls a pair of pants, a T Shirt, and walking shoes from a bag he had stashed in his car that morning before going to work.

> He quickly changes his clothes in the garage and scoops up the picnic basket and a blanket. His firm movement in closing the garage door transmits his energy and enthusiasm to Mary. It tells her that their real day starts now. The sounds of this arrival, that is at the same time a departure, floats suggestively over the neighborhood. It is unusual afternoon music in the corner where they live. The day is overcast but Mary's expression seems to say, "Pretty nice weather. We don't need coats!" – A great forecast John buys into as he opens the roof of the convertible. The sound of a happy motor and a happy tune

on the radio accompanies two smiling faces setting off for a happy afternoon escape.

Their walk through the countryside until sunset is a mindful meditation on the beauty of nature. They return home totally relaxed and with the feeling of having spent a long and exciting day together. Why cut a good thing short? Why not turn a nice afternoon into a great evening? So that's what they did. They prepared an exotic dinner, and the spices shared at the table inspired what naturally followed, until they fell asleep in each other's arms around midnight.

The day ended up being a cascade of exiting and fulfilling moments that counteracted a negative beginning marked by routine boredom and a lack of inspiration at work. John and Mary could develop an endless list of remedies for beating mid-week boredom and stress: shared activities such as cooking courses, joint fitness classes or an evening out dancing. These days would turn into good weeks and good months, until finally they looked back on a good year of exciting moments spent mastering the art of living.

If a long day of boring routine has left us low-spirited and tired, this scenario is not so likely to happen often, but it's a big risk to give in to a boring, routine evening after a boring, routine day. This is the moment to shake off the "usual" and opt for a healthy alternative to a life of 24 hour tedium. Being able to do this very much depends on our own mindset and attitude. We will deal with this topic in depth and see how with the right mindset and a few minutes of effort, we can create those hours of happiness and fulfillment that are the key to positively transforming our day.

Let's imagine another scenario. Let's turn our attention to the millions of people who have interesting jobs. These are people who should wake up every morning aware of the privilege of having a challenging, but exciting, day ahead; individuals who have every reason to start the morning in a good mood, enjoying their morning tea or coffee with the morning news before heading out to the inspiring, stimulating, well-paid work they will do in an affirming environment that acknowledges their contribution.

A cascade of good feelings day after day, month after month: a scenario that promises vitality the whole year through. But even these people have to be careful. A day well lived does not end with a good day at the office. What happens, or doesn't happen, afterward can change everything.

Let's imagine the arrival home of one of these millions who, at the first glance, seem to be irrefutably privileged persons. Let's follow Carla as she comes home.

Carla opens the garage door with a click of her remote control. Her little dog runs to greet her, wagging his tail and jumping up and down with happiness. But it seems there is no one at home except "Buddy" the dog. As usual, nobody is waiting to greet her. When she enters the living room, Mark drags itself slowly from the sofa and pushes the remote control button to lower the sound of the television. The soccer game goes on, as usual, and although he has lowered the volume, the man's attention continues to be glued to the game. This does permit Carla to ask the routine question: "How was your day?" and for Mark to give the routine answer: "As usual!" "What should we have dinner," Carla asks as she drops her heavy bag on the sofa and Mark answers, "I don't know. It doesn't matter. Whatever you want– the usual." Carla is still remembering the extraordinary lunch she enjoyed earlier that day at Culinary Fusion Art, one of the newest and most creative restaurants in town.

The usual TV dinners they ate in front of the TV screen constituted, as usual, a routine of stuffing the stomach that was light years away from enjoying a meal or sharing the table together. This set the tone for yet another boring evening, so boring, that the next morning neither one of them could remember who went to bed first alone and who fell asleep in front of the TV.

Carla's day ended up being a cascade of boring moments that annulled the excitement and satisfaction of what had gone before. We may have exaggerated a bit in this scenario. In many cases, if the longest part of the day has been exciting, there is a greater chance that some positive inspiration is going to carry over and make up for the boredom of the rest. Unfortunately, this is not always a guarantee. Each person's situation is different, and each life is as unique as the many minutes and seconds of the days, weeks, months, and years one is given to live. What is guaranteed, however, is that everyone having an average life span of 70 or 80 years has the possibility to live millions of unique moments and to experience millions of unusual exciting little things that beat the routine and banish boredom. The key to this process is in our own minds.

What "As Usual" things usually produce in a "Usual" society

In our industrialised world, robots are becoming ever more efficient in repetitiously carrying out the same task perfectly. They are the apotheosis of routine. However, we are not yet (and hopefully we will never become) robots. Robots can produce cars, make electronic equipment, package products, operate machines, and many other things. They have taken over many reception desk jobs because they have already learned to do most call center functions in many languages. They can clean our houses, swimming pools, and streets and will soon make our beds and prepare our dinner. Who knows if and when they might assume more intimate roles in our lives: never tired at the end of the day, never protesting, and nurtured with just a bit of electricity.

Robots are content to do the same job all day long and they never make mistakes! Their performance might inspire technocrats and bureaucrats and eventually seduce them with the possibility of getting things done without losing even a second due to human inefficiency. Robots would certainly save them the trouble of negotiating with trade unions and dealing with other authorities. They are indifferent to programmed routine and are paragons of obedience and loyalty.

What happens if we become robots and our blood is substituted by electronic impulses travelling through a network of wires and our brain cells act like Intel chips? We will have lost the use of our senses and will have become a part of the routine without achieving the perfection of a robot and without its inexhaustible 24 hour "work ethic".

So we must never adopt a robot mentality, and we should definitely prepare our minds to confront the routine and the world's attempts to program our lives. We should strive to be "**the Unusual**" intellectual and emotional commanders-in-chief who ensure that the human brain controls the amazing 21st technology which it inspired and created.

The day our minds and souls get decoded by a robot, robots will instantly replace the human species.

I 'm not trying to put forth the idea that the unbelievable advances made by great thinkers and entrepreneurs have not contributed favourably in many ways to our quality of life. I, myself, have a hearty affinity for papyrus and ink, but I am very well aware that writing this book would have been three times harder to do without the technological inventions of modern day information and communications geniuses. Nevertheless, I am fully aware that the inspiration to write the book came from my deeply-rooted analogue characteristics. My non-digital organs and senses made it happen.

We can't allow our hearts and minds to become infected by "Robot mania". Robots do not change their jobs until they are given instructions to do so. They are obedient and have no problems with the routine or with changes in their programming. They are immune to boredom and open to change as long their hardware and software are suited or adapted to the job they are assigned to carry out.

How different we are as human beings. On the job routine can reduce our attention span to dangerous levels. According to research, routine jobs involving automation are accountable for a high percentage of labour accidents. Routine has the same effect as a drug: the moment a person is abruptly deprived of it, he or she can become nervous and stressed. The addiction of routine can block our minds to change. Changing well-established habits is normally a step-by-step process, and forcing this process carries the risk of increasing our resistance to the point that we give up and return to the safe haven of life "as usual". Our initial relief in returning to the same old rut is short-lived. Again, we glumly face the high tide of routine and boredom. The real opportunity for transforming the boredom of the status quo lies in the process of empowering our minds for change. It's a question of creating many little inspirations that lead to extraordinary, exciting moments.

Our minds generate the inspiration for extraordinary little excitements

It's no secret that the power of our mind is the greatest power we possess.

Thousands of great books have been written about this subject from scientific, spiritual, and religious perspectives. Our minds can cure our bodies. The mind lifts a stone before the hand does. Our minds make things happen if we really want them to happen. They are the world's greatest warehouses of information and feelings. The real capacity of our mind continues to be one of the most exciting themes of science, philosophy, spirituality and the arts. Some of the latest fields of scientific research are dedicated to decoding our brainwaves with the goal of endowing computers with human response mechanisms not dependent upon speech or body movement.

From the ancient Greek philosophers who had a strong affinity for the power and mystery of our minds until the computerised 21st century, the human mind has determined our conceptions of life and the afterlife. There will always be differing opinions and interpretations, but there has been a consensus for thousands of years over three aspects of the mind:

A positive mind, an open mind, and **an active mind** are the tremendous and unlimited sources of the inspirations we need to project feelings, ideas, and projects .Taking it to the limit: If we were always inspired by our minds, we would **NEVER HAVE A DULL MOMENT**. It seems to be paradox. Never before in history have we enjoyed such an array of novel, external stimulations to amuse us. The world of digital communication, and the tremendously improved opportunities for leisure travel for hundreds of millions of people, should theoretically signify the end of boredom. Unfortunately, this has not been the case.

Many minds are hungry for excitement. They crave it even without being able to read, understand, or digest the greatest menu of anti-boredom delights ever offered in all of history. It is said that only ten percent of our mind's capacity is used, and that even this small percent is not always used efficiently. If this is true, it is a tremendous waste in a world where the offer of stimulus is almost unlimited and efficiency is so highly rated. But let's take a positive approach to this situation for a moment, and look at the mind's inefficiency and the ten percent utilization rate of our rational and emotional resources as an opportunity. The mind reserves space for those individuals who want to expand their quotas of inspiration and creative ideas and we need to generate more inspiration and more creative ideas if we want to counter balance deadening routines and energy-sapping boredom.

The reader who agrees with the simple logic of these observations would, in principle, not be resistant to being open-minded if it meant getting more out of life. Remember, 90 percent of our mind is not being used. Top your lap top with your mind top. You deserve the best. Let's start advancing toward a positive state of mind!

The unique TRIPLE MIND ALLIANCE:

A positive Mind -An open Mind - An active Mind
   (The Alliance against routine and boredom)

A positive Mind

A positive Mind is the entrance door to good feelings

We all have family members, friends, and business relations who have, or who we perceive as having, a very negative or very positive overall attitude. Who amongst them are the happiest? This question answers itself.

Negativists believe the world will end tomorrow and they are certainly right when it comes to their own personally-perceived world. If you only expect disaster, it will most likely be waiting for you at the corner, just as expecting good fortune is apt to bring luck your way. Predisposition aside, whether disaster strikes or good luck comes whistling will greatly depend upon your actions. Throughout history, individuals with a positive attitude have inspired the energy, passion, and hope needed to move our world forward in its most critical moments.

Positive thinkers have pushed human progress forward, while negativists, when they weren't dismantling the progress already made, have tended to hold it back.

In his book *Emotional Intelligence*, Daniel Goleman underlines the power of positive thinking (positivism, optimism, and hope, an inseparable trio). Positive thinking is having strong expectations that, in general, things will turn out all right in one's life.

Negative emotions and feelings cannot always be avoided. Fate can deal us hard times and even temporarily bring us close to desperation. We can unexpectedly find ourselves being the object of pity. But the pity of others is normally not enough to pull us out of a well of despair. In very trying times, the insight and understanding of others and their re-motivating support are what really count. The worst sentiment we can embrace is self-pity. It is the worst advisor we can listen to when it comes to our moods. We need to use the full power of our mind when we are down. The gas pedal of our positive energy has to be pushed to the limit and there is no doubt that a positive mood fires up our rockets of positive feelings and prepares us for a new take-off. The world goes forward and we need go forward with it.

Positivism is a natural gift that some individuals enjoy from birth, but even those who have not had this genetic luck, or whose life circumstances have marred their ability to feel happy, still have the opportunity to develop a positive mind.

There are hundreds of interesting books written on the topic, but their essence can be summed up in these three gems of advice:

1) Life is a wonder and worth living. So live it!

(Life is full of opportunities. If we earnestly seek them, we will find them.)

2) Consider every problem as not just a problem, but as an opportunity as well.

(Every problem presents an opportunity to learn, to act, and to change.)

3) Never give up hope. Reach out and do everything in your power to create a better future.

(Throughout history there are many examples of people who have learned how to "attract good luck".)

Positivists smile more and are happier

To be positive, we have to master the art of smiling and practice it often. A smile is infectious and spreads happiness. If we draw a picture of a smiling little girl and ask children what the picture is about, nine out of ten will say, "A happy girl!"

If we ask someone to give us a synonym for happiness, he is very likely to say, "A smile". I would say that he was right, even though I know that I'll never find smile listed as a synonym for happiness in any thesaurus. There is, without a doubt, a proportional relationship between the how much we smile and the frequency of our positive moods and our state of happiness. If we had a smile meter in our body and could read the results, it would be easy to determine a smile's effect on how happy we feel ourselves to be.

In some cultures and business environments, people are trained to smile. To those who would say that this is an artificial method, I would suggest that they teach their people not to smile and then observe the results.

One of the first lessons I learned travelling around the world is that economic prosperity is not the determining factor in whether or not people smile a lot. I can't count how many unsmiling faces I have seen in the shadows of glamorous skyscrapers, proud totems of a flourishing economy. It was most likely that the stress visible on those faces was due these people's monotonous daily routines, boredom, and de-motivating working and living situations. Although their pockets where full, their happiness tank was running on empty.

I have seen many spontaneous and natural smiles on the faces of people living under hard conditions, as well as many unhappy faces of people who could no longer summon the energy to smile. The capacity to smile had been driven out them by the un-human conditions they were forced to live in. Small-minded negativists who live in prosperous countries would immediately say: "It's poverty, misery, and their own laziness which makes them unhappy. Sure, we are blessed to have been born in a prosperous country, but our happiness didn't come by itself! We had to work hard for it!" Based on my experience, they are indulging in unfounded, discriminatory judgements made without factual evidence.

If we could scientifically measure the deep down collective happiness of many of those so-called underprivileged societies and compare it to that of wealthier societies, we would be surprised at the outcome. Our mood barometer would tell us that high levels of material wealth do not necessarily produce real happiness.

Often, easily-achieved wealth contributes to high incidences of boredom, lack of inspiration, unproductive routines, or unrealistic aspirations. If driven by unchecked desires, what was once a healthy "spice of life" can evolve into a debilitating vice that eats away at us behind a false facade of happiness.

Having made the above comments and observations, I am far from claiming that socio-economically developed societies, whose citizens enjoy access to balanced nutrition, a good education, and an advanced level of democracy, are not a more fertile ground for overall collective happiness. It should not be a secret to well-informed people however, that in the most advanced countries of the world there are more suicides than in the less-developed parts of our planet, particularly among children and young people.

There is no greater disaster for parents than losing a son or daughter to suicide. Having to come to grips with the devastating fact that their child believed that life wasn't worth living anymore and to live with the guilt that they were not able to prevent the tragedy must be almost unbearable.

The simplest way of discovering the positive state of mind and collective happiness of a community is to look into the eyes of its children and its elderly people. If the light of happiness is in their eyes, there is happiness in the heart of the community. As for the people in the middle age group of these communities, although they are not free of the daily problems we all face, from the happiness demonstrated by their elders and their children, they must be managing life's realities well.

Gross Domestic Happiness versus Gross Domestic Product

There are different ways of interpreting wealth. One is the economic standard denominated the **GDP** (Gross Domestic Product), which considers the market value of all goods and services produced by a nation in a given year. Another concept of measuring a nation's wealth is the **GDH** (Gross Domestic Happiness), utilized in the small Himalayan nation of Bhutan since 1972 that considers the overall state of wellbeing of that country's people.

Some great day in the future all world leaders should learn to compare the GDP with the **GDH.** I would even vote for measuring wealth by the still better concept of the **NDH** (Net Domestic Happiness).

I personally have observed that there is a relevant difference between the standard of living and quality of life. The ideal mix is most likely a national policy that seeks a balance between the economic means necessary to live well and the right to the personal time an individual requires to maintain a happy family life and to cultivate his or her inner self.

The state of our minds determines our real happiness

I'd like to share a personal travel anecdote. Once I took a trip that started out in a grey and rainy Western European country, sharing a traffic jam on the way to the airport with a particularly morose taxi driver with a bored expression on his face. A long night and a morning later, my plane touched down in Madras, (today Chennai) India.

With my last ounce of energy and in an average mood, I claimed my luggage and climbed into a nearby taxi. The air was so thick that you could have cut it with a knife and so hot that I felt sorry for the birds in the trees. The oppressive atmosphere was dragging down both my body and mind, but the taxi driver's upbeat attitude began to lift my mood. For me, this taxi driver was one of those great examples of how one person's positive attitude can spread exponentially in seconds and positively affect another person's state of mind for days. He left me with a positive mood that would last my whole stay in Madras. The following poem I wrote sums up the ride and what I got out of it:

Sunny Dialogue
Today, it is a sunny day!
"Yes Sir, that's here normally the way
The way the heaven deals with us:
Many, many, sunny days and just a bit of a rush.
A little less as in your country is it not right?
You are right and happy Sir and that is bright!
(Madras, now Chennai 03-11-99)

Taxi drivers, I found out, are interesting references when you want to make an on-the-spot mood check. They are, in fact, double mood meters. The first mood meter is their personal mood that is very often shared by their fellow taxi-drivers. If over time you end up travelling the same route between an airport and a city, and all the taxi drivers who pick you up are either bored or in a bad mood, you can be certain that there is a correlation between their personal bad moods and the general mood of the communities they are you driving in and out of.

The second mood meter is, unfortunately, related to the real taxi meter registering the mounting expense of your trip. If the taxi driver is driving you around as though you had asked for a tour of the city sights, he is definitely in the mood to cheat you. I found out about this particular mood by trial and error in many different cities and learned to be alert and negotiate prices and destinations beforehand, when necessary.

My taxi driver in Madras no doubt had to endure a hard daily life just to put bread on the family table, but he did his job with a smile and a positive attitude. He made me feel positive too, and opened my mind and my heart.

What you see in the Mood Mirror

Being aware of our moods is essential in maintaining a vital state of mind. Remember the old wisdom about taking an honest look at ourselves in the mirror every morning? When we look at ourselves in the mirror we normally give ourselves a very critical going over. Who is perfect, physically or mentally? Nobody! It's also a good exercise to take an honest look at the state of mind we see reflected in the mirror every morning, with the understanding that no one can be forever in the best of moods.

Our moods fluctuate according to many interrelated internal and external factors that include our overall physical and mental health, the dynamics of our relationships, our work environment, and current socio-political and economic climates. Moods can be greatly affected by the seasons and weather conditions. In northern regions, short dark winter days and a rainy climate can create individual seasonal affective disorders that evolve into a collective passive melancholy. In places where climate has a strong adverse effect on one's wellbeing, it's of crucial importance to ward off negativity with UV treatments and to make a concerted effort to kindle the inner light and joy of our hearts and minds.

The mood mirror can do miracles. Imagine looking at yourself in a mirror. The mirror doesn't lie and your heart confirms that that you are not really happy. You ask yourself why you are in a bad mood and you decide that it must be the weather. Today the rain is coming down in buckets, just as it has for days, or even weeks, on end. You could ask yourself if it isn't, in fact, good fortune that it's raining. Where you are, everything outside is lush and green and the rain will assure an abundant harvest, while at the same moment in some other parts of the world, the wells are empty and people are starving and dying of thirst. It's clear that these types of situations can, and should be, managed through positive thinking.

Someone who complains too much about the rain has never longed for a simple glass water just to survive.

Imagine looking into the mirror again, this time with an expression of happiness on your face. You and your former negative mood appear to be completely transformed. That's what a mirror reflection can do! Modern research has shown that the act of making positive facial expressions in a mirror provides immediate positive feedback to the inner mind that stimulates a positive mood shift. So it makes sense to engage your mirror in a positive dialogue every morning.

There are stronger reasons for having a bad mood than a rainy day, but believe me, if you have the will to be in the good mood, through a positive outlook you'll find the motives to change the expression reflected in your mirror.

A positive mind helps us to be happier people and happiness should be everyone's goal in life. But happiness is not a destination; it's a way of living and an objective we can achieve if we learn how to manage our moods and to practice happiness.

Happiness experienced in the past is a reservoir of happiness for the future

It seems to be a law of nature and destiny that life has its ups and downs. Without the low points there are no high points. In this sense, life functions like an alternating electrical current. If we are wise, we make a habit of building up our savings in financially good years as a hedge against more difficult times. We should do the same with our emotional happiness, because the fulfilling happy moments we have lived constitute a reservoir of happiness that can nurture our hearts when the cold winds of adversity blow. Managing our moods is a question of emotional intelligence and practical wisdom.

If we learn to have a positive attitude about such simple things as rainy days, we can fill our emotional well and drink deeply from it during those inevitable dry spells. Just like a sophisticated modern solar system that stores energy to brighten our lives when the sun doesn't shine, we can store positive memories that will give us the energy to face difficult moments. A positive and grateful nature that appreciates good moments in the past is better prepared to deal with whatever the future might bring.

If we don't know how to benefit from our personal happiness reservoir and instead are always striving desperately for bigger and better things, we aren't being realistic and are on the fast track toward desperation and disillusionment. A very old Chinese proverb says, "Happiness is appreciating what you have and not looking desperately for what you do not have." This proverb is not advice to give up hope for better times or not do one's utmost to make them happen. It is simply the observation that a person who does not recognize and appreciate the good things in his present and his past will forever search for an elusive perfect happiness, a voyage that will inevitably end with the perception that the past has been nothing more than a long succession of boring unsatisfactory moments devoid of joy and excitement.

A positive mind contributes to the development of an open mind and an open mind is a determining factor in developing an active mind. The Triple Mind Alliance: Positive Mind, Open Mind, and Active mind, is a unique, synergizing, energizing, and inspiring trio that beats the routine and boredom we often passively fall into and helps us to forge more exciting lives. Let's move ahead and get to know the central and most important member of the Triple Mind Alliance: The Open Mind.

An Open Mind

Open your mind and download (almost) everything you like.

Don't worry that your mind might get overcharged. Our mind has a tremendous scanning capability and there is no risk of completely filling it up. The average person utilizes only 10 percent of his brain's capacity. **Your mind tops the latest laptop in the market.** An open mind takes pleasure in scanning information because it is naturally tuned into a simple cyber principle: without input there is no output. The open mind scans so that the active mind can interpret, create ideas, and revel in emotions. Even more importantly, it can scan qualitatively, basing its search on our personal affinities and what we consider to be of value. The quality of what we feed our minds will greatly determine the quality of our thoughts. As the saying goes, it's "Garbage In, Garbage Out".

An open Mind is the entrance door to unlimited perceptions.

Think about the following proverb:

> "An open mind always leaves a space for someone to drop a worthwhile thought in it"

Can you imagine the number of intelligent and wise people that we might meet during our lifetimes who could drop worthwhile thoughts into our minds? I can tell you that I appreciate every worthwhile drop that comes my way. The more drops that sink in, the more we realize how little we know and how many life-enriching things we still can learn.

I wish knowledge and wisdom would not only come to me drop by drop, but that they would rain freely into my open mind.

Children have an open mind. Unfortunately, childhood is short and a child's socialization, that imparts so many prejudices, makes it even shorter. This is a preoccupying situation in societies where education is little more than indoctrination. Navigating through the digital world, I landed on the following statement worth sharing:

> "The world is full of people who have never, since childhood, met an open doorway with an open mind."

It's a real pity that the virgin minds of our children are walled off from so much useful and life-inspiring knowledge and wisdom that could serve them their entire lives and be a heritage that they transmit to the next generation.

All children should have a fair chance to develop their own unique personality in synchronicity with the particular moment in time in which they were born. Children need to be more than just happy. They need to be prepared to surpass the experiences and the achievements of their parents' generation. The great Lebanese-American artist, poet, and writer Khalil Gibran expressed this beautifully:

"Your children are not your children. They are the sons and the daughters of Life's longing for itself. They come through you not from you and though they are with you, yet they belong not to you. You may give them your love but not your thoughts for they have their own thoughts. You may house their bodies but not their souls..."

Most of our opinions are prejudices acquired through the process of socialization. Even if we are exposed to new ways of thinking and new points of view later in life, it is hard for us to cast off the baggage of the one-dimensional society that first nurtured us. We tend to construct our beliefs and truths upon our own cultural frameworks. This isn't a problem as long as we don't presume exclusive ownership of the truth and come to believe that the billions of other human beings born in other parts of this planet were unlucky not to have been born into our particular society. Over-socialization leads to dogmatic points of view and is a form of mental incest. It closes the mind with an iron-clad door and locks it away from so much that could enrich a life.

The more I have travelled, the more travel has opened my mind. Driven by curiosity, but moved by a deep respect for other points of view, I have progressively learned to get more out of each new journey. Travel has increased my tolerance and sharpened my views, but it has not meant throwing away all the thoughts and convictions my parents and my community instilled in me as a youth. Respecting the thoughts of others does not imply that we have to share them. Respect is tolerance, sharing is conviction or conversion. The only absolute truth is physical death. One person's truth might be, for example, what he finds for himself in terms of his inner and outer peace. The following poem seeks to illustrate the quintessence of the relativity of truth:

"World Lesson"
I travelled all my life. All the globe around with all the passion found.
I met many minds and faces from cultures and from races.
Most of them inspiring, some of them concerning
But all of them gave me ONE GREAT LEARNING:
Nothing is absolutely true. Minds should be open for a shift.
That is without doubt my greatest travel gift.
IB 3734 Madrid- Cairo 18-10-2008

The open mind and our senses

An open mind is an attitude. The phrase "to be open-minded" is frequently bandied about to describe someone because it sounds positive. Most people like to be perceived as being open- minded. However, being open-minded is often erroneously interpreted as being open to virtually everything.

In only a few seconds, an Internet search engine can churn out a list of thousands of websites that offer us new, unlimited sources of information and opinions that we can instantly download onto **our private hard and heart disks.** The same principle applies to all other sources of information and the entire environment that surrounds us, whether our source is the media, the street, school, or the workplace. Our mind is grateful for assistance in determining the quantity and quality of what we download, because not everything is worth recording and digesting. Our education, our intellect, and our senses will help us to download with common sense.

Our senses are our main support system for scanning, filtering, and recording what our open minds are offered. Our **senses of sight, hearing, smell, taste, and touch** comprise the communications system that connects our bodies and our minds. Without our senses, we would be lost. We wouldn't be able to move from one place to another, protect ourselves against danger, or communicate. Without the aid of our senses, our minds would be empty. But our senses are now becoming seriously blunted. From the times when Homo sapiens wore a loin-skin and sought shelter in caves to the present, our senses have been progressively losing their acuity. The reasons for this are simple and logical. What you do not use, you lose. Thanks to scientific advances, we have progressively relied less and less on our senses, and as a result, much of our sensorial capacity has atrophied. When our forefathers slept in their caves, they had no light except on those nights when the full moon cast a modest beam. To perceive danger and protect themselves against predators or human enemies, they had to rely on all their senses. When our ancestors went looking for food, they needed sharp eyes, an excellent sense of hearing, and a keen sense of smell to meet their daily needs. Their senses never evolved to be as sharp as those of the animals and reptiles of their time, but they were definitely more acute than ours are now.

It was Homo sapiens' capacity to think that gave him an equal chance of survival. This thinking capacity has permitted us to progress materially, but with every new material comfort we have invented we have relied less upon our senses to survive and our sensorial capacity has greatly deteriorated. Of course, we have every reason to be grateful for material progress. Today we have communication systems we could not even have dreamed about only 25 years ago, but like many other scientific innovations, they further erode our sensorial abilities. It seems that scientific and material progress play an evolutionary role in mankind's destiny that we must be aware of and counter balance.

We would be dogmatically blind and deaf to consider ourselves the "ultimate Homo sapiens" because we are the masters of advanced technology. It would be an error to consider ourselves technically perfect beings that do not need sharp ears because we have multiple electronic warning systems and sound amplifying chips or that we can do without sharp eyes because we have prescription glasses and amplifying electronic lenses. Who needs a sharp sense of smell when we have an entire industry dedicated to creating strong fragrances identified by our noses in seconds, you might ask? Of what use are highly developed senses if we can delegate the greater part of their functions to modern technology? Our brain should be happy to have less work decoding and interpreting so many stimuli and shouldn't complain!

Fortunately, our brain instinctively knows the truth and doesn't feel very good about it. We all know deep down that what you do not use, you lose, and in some faraway corner of our minds lurks the fear that one day human beings could find themselves bereft of sensorial skills. The human mind is now becoming aware of the possible consequences of over-delegating its sensorial responsibilities to external hardware and software.

Imagine one day no longer being able to see the beauty of a flower and smell its fragrance, or not being able to hear the breath of your baby lying next to you. Imagine not seeing the contours of another's lips approaching yours in the shadows or feeling the soft touch of a kiss. Imagine not smelling the bread burning in your toaster, or the gas leak in your kitchen, or not hearing your smoke detector wailing until, finally, its battery went dead. What will happen if we stop smelling the gases belching out of factory chimneys and the exhaust systems of cars or the strange smell of the rotting plants and trees that died because we were deaf to their cry for survival?

What our brain is telling us makes a lot of sense: we must keep our senses alive because they help us to protect ourselves and get more out of life.

Awakening and supercharging our Senses

Enrich your mind with nature's knowledge

Human beings and animals alike rely on their senses to perceive and interact with the world around them. But animals have more senses than human beings, and their senses have always been more highly developed. Furthermore, animals have never lost sensorial acuity by delegating their sensorial functions to technology, as man has done.

Mother Nature was well aware of the need to equip the animal world with more highly developed senses in order to help one species to survive beside another and to protect all species of animals from the human species, whose thinking mind, hungry stomach, and need for protection against hungry animals made him a fearsome enemy.

Their superior sensorial capacity was the animal world's good fortune. Although man developed a powerful array of weapons to hunt animals, his inferior senses slowed the hunt considerably, preventing the total annihilation of many species. Unfortunately, many species have vanished from the planet forever and many others are in danger, an example of an unforgivable crime perpetrated by man against nature.

There are still a lot of secrets to be learned about the senses of animals and scientists continue to study them. What scientists are learning now could one day compensate in small part for the environmental disaster that man has created and help animals to survive in their increasingly effected and deteriorated habitats. This work could also benefit mankind's own wellbeing.

A fascinating sensory capability unique to the animal kingdom is the ability to detect incipient abnormal electro-magnetic wave movements. The Greek historian Diodoro Siculo observed this phenomenon as early as 50 B.C., noting that mice and snakes left cities before an earthquake.

Almost a quarter of a million people caught by surprise by the disastrous East Asian tsunami in 2004 lost their lives. The loss of fauna was much less, due to the animals' sensorial pre-warning system that gave them time move to safer ground. It is a pity that human beings have lost the habit of observing the behavior of the wildlife that surrounds them. In the case of the 2004 tsunami, simple observation could have saved thousands of human lives. Let's take a closer look at the creatures that share our planet and discover some of the many things we can learn from them.

Seeing like a hawk

The sense of sight is the human's most important sense, as it counts for approximately eighty percent of our sensory perceptions. One either becomes a bit jealous or very respectful when he compares his vision with the spatial and visual acuity of a hawk.

Nobody questions the notion that a bird's angle of vision is broader than a human being's. We frequently use the metaphor "bird's eye view" in our daily conversations to describe a broader picture of something, and it's often said that someone with good long-distance vision, or of someone who is a keen observer, that he "has eyes like a hawk". A hawk's eyesight is eight times more powerful than a human's. This powerful vision allows him to see a mouse in a field one mile away. If he could only read, he could peruse a newspaper from a height equivalent to a seven-storey building with no problem! Our modern radar systems can track an object the size of a bird fifty miles away, but unfortunately, our eyes are not individually equipped with million dollars of defense technology. That's not the last word concerning the hawk's superior vision. Swooping at a speed of up to 120 miles per hour from a great height, he never loses his focus on the prey he is tracking.

We will never have a hawk's eyesight, but we can definitely learn to see the broader picture without losing our focus on the details. Both professional and amateur photographers love their zoom lenses, but every one of us should have his own inner mental zoom to capture and record the astonishing and exciting moments we live.

Hearing like a mouse

Mice need a sharp sense of hearing to be safe from cats. In real life, the virtuosity of a mouse's auditory system is much more amazing than the antics of his cartoon counterparts in a Walt Disney movie.

Hearing, also known as audition, is the perception of movements of air waves measured in Hertz frequencies. The average human can hear frequencies ranging from 12 to 20,000 Hz. A mouse has a range five times greater than a human being, and can detect frequencies from 1,000 to 100,000 Hz. This range enables it to hear the approach of the most silent of enemies. We will never have a mouse's auditory range, but can learn to listen more and learn more by listening.

Smelling like a bee

Smelling the unlimited fragrances of the world is exciting and a particular pleasure when it comes to the fragrances of the flowers. We are drawn to flowers "like a bee to honey" as the saying goes. Bees however, do not to need to stick their noses into a flower to capture its fragrance. They can perceive its perfume from miles away. We will never have their capacity to enjoy a rose from such a distance but we can add more pleasure to our lives if we make it a habit to "take time out to smell the roses".

Discriminating tastes like a rabbit

There is no doubt that our sense of taste is one of our most important senses. Closing our eyes to concentrate tastes on our tongue, we put 9000 taste buds in action that send potent messages to our mind. Our taste buds tell us when the wine is exquisite, the chocolate is divine, or the coffee is bitter. They can even alert us that the cheese is rancid or the fish is suspiciously "too fishy" and might give us a nasty case of food poisoning. A rabbit, with 15,000 taste buds, is a discriminating gourmet that must really enjoy his diet of carrots and greens. Rabbits we will never be, but we neither should ever wrinkle our noses at carrots and greens. We should take inspiration from our fuzzy gourmet friends and savor every flavor of life, from the first fresh-squeezed orange juice in the morning to the last good night kiss at night.

Feeling like a cat

We all have childhood memories of warmth and security transmitted to us through the sense of touch. We refer to the thrill of a kiss and other emotional highs registered through the sense of touch as a "touching experiences". We feel the sun, the rain, and the wind and have we have learned to dress according to the changes in the weather and the seasons, although modern air conditioning and heating systems have ruptured our bodies' natural relationships with the seasonal cycles and changes in the weather. However, we maintain an ever-increasing distance with nature and our fellow human beings. How often in talking about old schoolmates, colleagues, and even family members, we say that "we've fallen out of touch," or "we haven't been in touch for a long time."

In modern societies that value individual ambition more than tribal consensus and revel in virtual contact via internet, we have lost our sense of the tactile and our ancient predisposition to touch and be touched. In the 1970s Desmond Morris wrote about this crisis in our intimate behavior:

> "Unhappily, and almost without noticing it, we have gradually become less and less touchful, more and more distant, and physical untouchability has been accompanied by emotional remoteness"

All of a cat's senses are highly developed, but its sense of touch is truly remarkable. Cats use their whiskers to navigate and make spatial judgments, quite literally "feeling their way around" the world. Their radar-like whiskers are sensitive enough to detect the slightest change in the movement of the air around them, which is bad news for the mice they stalk, and they use them to measure entry room before they cram themselves into impossibly tight spaces. The sensitivity of feline tactile hairs was so appreciated by the inventors of early crystal radio sets that they dubbed the contact wire of their new invention "the cat's whiskers". The angle of a cat's whiskers is a reliable indicator of his mood. If he wears them extended forward, you can assume that he is happy and relaxed. If he pulls them back at a sharp angle it indicates that he is probably "touchy" and might scratch or bite.

We could emulate our feline friends by trying to develop more sensitivity to subtle shifts in the environment around us and learning how not to barge into situations where we might not, either literally or figuratively, "fit in". Most of all, we can learn how to overcome the physical untouchability and emotional remoteness so well described by Desmond Morris, and so endemic to modern societies, from observing how cats use their sense of touch in their social relations with other felines and with humans.

Our senses influence our moods and contribute to our wellness. They deserve the greatest attention and care because they provide us with 24 hour protection and it is through them that we perceive the world.

Many years ago I came across a wonderful children's book *We are Wolves* that described how a family of wolves used their senses to survive. In this delightful story, "Uncle Wolf" introduces two young cubs to the world, teaching them all about being wolves. In the story, they learn to be watchers, listeners, travelers, and hunters as their mother proudly watches their progress. But most important of all, they learn about their pack and being a family.

My kids loved the book, and they asked for it again and again for months on end. I loved it too, and after reading it many times with my children, I became a bit more like a wolf myself, watching, listening, travelling, and hunting new ideas. Sharing this book with my kids gave me the wonderful feeling of being a child again.

Who wouldn't like to have the sensorial superiority of all these animals? If we cultivate our senses more, we will be more aware of the beauty of everything around us, the dangers we must avoid, and the million opportunities for happiness that we have never noticed before. **So let's see like hawk, hear like a mouse, smell like a bee, discriminate what we taste like a rabbit, feel like a cat, and think as a human being.**

Learn from farmers & fishermen

It is not surprising that those who live with nature learn from nature.

Farmers and fishermen live with nature and harvest its bounty. Keen observers, their profound knowledge of nature and close relationship with it are the most important elements of their work and the greatest source of their satisfaction with what they do for a living. From dawn until dusk and often through the night, farmers and fisherman live in the original Eden and experience it in all its cycles and in every kind of weather. They see, hear, smell, taste, and feel all of nature's permutations more intensely than others. Like the creatures around them, they use their senses to anticipate changes in the weather, predict good and bad harvests, or find fertile fishing grounds. For the sake of our senses, we should all be a farmer or a fisherman in one moment or another of our lives.

Learn from the artists and craftsmen

Where do artists and craftsmen find their inspiration? They cultivate a higher sensitivity to the world around them than the average person. They are more attuned to the infinite variety and beauty of nature. Creative people have more than the usual affinity for the pleasure of smelling, tasting, feeling, and touching. They sharpen, train, and indulge their senses to interpret their perceptions in unlimited, different, and personal ways. The 18th century realist painter Wilhelm Leibl made a succinct statement about the capacity to observe meticulously: "It is all about seeing the things that the majority does not see." The amazing paintings of the contemporary Iranian painter Iman Maleki, perhaps the world's greatest living master of realism, show an almost divine arousal of the artist's senses. The details of his paintings are so finely rendered that they seem alive and are a demonstration of an incredible level of artistic expression.

Not everybody can become a renowned artist but every person ever born has by nature at least one special talent. There is a hidden artist in each of us. If we refine our senses like an artist does, we can discover our own unique gift for expression. Through which of our senses do we express our thoughts and feelings best?

If it is your sense of sight, you could interpret your visions in painting, drawing, or writing. If it is your sense of hearing, let the sounds of the world inspire you. Music could be your creative outlet, whether you decide to sing, play an instrument, or start dancing to the music and rhythm around you. If taste is your strongest sense, you could start exploring the world of gastronomy, cooking up surprises for yourself and others. If your greatest affinity is for feeling and touching, there are plenty of arts where sensitive fingers can learn the necessary skills to create works of art. Obviously, you might have several affinities and could become a multi- talented artist. You could do it just for fun or even have fun while making it pay!

Learn from children

The suggestion that we can learn a lot from children might provoke the response that children should learn a lot from adults. Both statements are true. There is no doubt that we learn from those having more knowledge and more experience, but what happens when the magical qualities we had as children get lost or forgotten in the process of growing up? The loss of the intense use of one's senses is one of saddest casualties in everyone's road to maturity.

You can warn a small child not to crawl where you have just dropped a needle, but whose sharp eyes are most likely to find the lost needle? While Dad searches for his glasses, Junior has already found it and picked it up from the carpet. Anyone who has told a story from what he assumed was a discreet distance from his son or daughter, only to hear it repeated later word for word, will never again question the sensitivity of a child's hearing. Both examples are proof of two things: that a child's senses are incredibly acute and that his curiosity has no limits. That's why our darling children behave a bit like little animals. They are guided by their natural curiosity, their wide-open eyes focus on every detail like a hawk, and they have the ears of a mouse when it comes to hearing what interests them. Like a bee, they smell something delicious miles away and they have a rabbit's finicky taste buds when it comes to deciding what they will eat and what they won't. Like a cat, they are usually inclined to cuddle and purr, but are also capable of biting and scratching when they are angry. Kids are open-minded and their senses endow them with a high level of creativity.

A healthy, happy, child's curiosity is stimulated by his finely-honed senses and curiosity is not just the mother of all knowledge and wisdom, it is the ultimate cure for boredom. The American writer Dorothy Parker made the following observation about curiosity:

"The cure for boredom is curiosity. There is no cure for curiosity."

A happy child playing is a one person theatre, acting and communicating with everything around him. Children talk to everything, from human beings and animals, to the objects they play with. To a child, everything is exciting; there is nothing that is not worth seeing, hearing, touching, smelling, playing with, or even biting into. If all this creative freedom were danger-free, we would never want to grow up at all. One of the greatest artists of the 20th century, the Spanish painter Pablo Picasso, summed up the natural creative talent of children when he said: "Every child is an artist. The problem is how to remain an artist once we grow up."

Let's learn from our kids. Recapturing a bit of childhood would revitalize our senses and teach us to observe and judge the world around us with a less-jaundiced eye. It would reopen the windows of our minds that society closed so long ago and let in some unpolluted mental oxygen. Children can remind us of the necessity for communicating honestly and openly and help us rediscover the daily excitement of living.

The senses love the seasons

Love is in the air. Spring is in the air! Birds sing, make their nests, and fill them with new life. More than just flowers bloom in the spring. It is the high season for our senses and there are more love stories made, written, composed, and sung in spring than in any other season of the year.

It does us good to fall a little bit in love with everything that is alive around us in spring. It is a time of personal revival and reawakening. It has been said that every April God rewrites the book of Genesis. Our senses love this season more than any other and reward us with many exciting feelings and blissful moments.

In summer, the abundance of light and warmth invites us to take off our clothes and dive naked as the day we were born into the waves of the ocean. Lying on our backs and looking up at the summer sky, our senses are fuelled by the closeness of our skin to our Mother Earth and our minds feel free and unfettered. Like a yearly tribal ritual, we celebrate the night campfire, the clear reflections in a mountain lake, or the wind that fill the sails of a skiff. Summer is the season of perfumed nights that seduce our grateful senses.

When green leaves turn to gold, nature signals us that the peak of the year's vitality is passing and that autumn, the season to harvest the summer's abundance, is at hand. Before winter closes in, our senses are assaulted by an onrush of tastes and colors. We are dazzled by the play of light and shadow in the landscape. A season to be grateful and count our blessings, we should treat every autumn day as if it were Thanksgiving Day.

Winter is the season when everything ends and begins again! No other season better represents and reflects the effect of seasonal changes on our senses and our mood. The touch of melancholy we feel is a common example. Our senses register the fading colors, the diminishing light, the drop in temperature, and the absence of fragrances. The earth seems to hide its vitality from us. It is a season to rest, repair, and prepare for the next outburst of spring.

Our five senses love the four seasons and if you make a habit of using your senses to enjoy each one, they will reward you with many exciting moments. Later on in this book you will find practical tips on how to add a little "seasoning" to your year.

"Yes but" versus "Why not?"

An open mind is, by definition, open to listening and thinking about new ideas and visions instead of blocking them out. New ideas can inspire us to experience new and exciting things, which is reason enough to be open-minded.

How often a proposal implying a change of mind or attitude is greeted the automatic reply: "Yes, but...", "Ja, aber...", "Oui, mais...", or "Si, pero...".

There is no language or culture where "but" does not frequently crop up when a change is suggested.

In fact, "but" is, a "no" nicely camouflaged by a "yes". "Yes, but" is a closed-mind reaction that has been responsible for delaying many projects, killing many ideas, blocking a lot of progress, and preventing a lot of change. A few years ago, I attended a business conference held to review a business plan with ambitious short mid-term objectives and to convince a group of managers that this plan could open up challenging new opportunities. A new senior manager was responsible for stirring up passion about the new plan that implied the need for a significant mind shift on the part of the existing established team. He made questioning the "Yes, but" attitude the focus of his pep talk and proposed substituting it with a pro-active "YES" attitude. He asked the team to respond to any new idea proposed during the conference with **"Why not?"** instead of "Yes, but" and the overall impact of his request was astonishing. Not one "Yes, but" cropped up during the rest of the conference and spirit of "Why not?", "Warum nicht?", "Pourqoi pas?", and "Porque no?" was not only taken to heart, but around the world. Given the human species' reluctance to change old ideas and habits, I'm not sure that "Yes, but" permanently disappeared from everyone's vocabulary, although all involved had made a good start! For an open mind, "Why not?" is an attitude worth adopting again and again. It definitely beats the "Yes, but" mindset as a starting point from which to move on to new, exciting, ideas.

We are the gatekeepers of what is downloaded into our minds

The impressive half century of scientific and technological progress made at the close of the last millennium equipped the world entering the 21st century with more opportunities to experience new and exciting sensory stimuli than in all the previous 20 centuries put together. For positive and open minds, we live in a moment that is ripe for opening our minds to new inspiration and exciting ideas. However, according to several studies, this unprecedented availability and easy access to novel stimuli has not prevented many people from suffering an unprecedented level of boredom.

It seems that the overwhelming variety we are offered has only speeded up what is known as the "wear out" effect. We suffer a constant, unfulfilled need for new external stimuli that appears to be the result of an uncontrolled mental greed and a failing mental capacity for fully digesting and enjoying new information and novelties.

S.J. Vodanovich, professor of psychology at the University of West Florida, has identified the reason for the dissatisfaction we experience in our search for enduring excitement as the absence of "Inner Amusement Skills":

> "In the absence of these inner amusement skills, the external world will always fail to provide enough excitement and novelty. "The brain is always seeking stimulation and over time it takes more and more. It's a losing battle. You just cannot get enough."

In responding to stimuli, we often tend to reject depth and over-focus on limited areas of information, missing the qualitative. The really mind-enriching information goes unnoticed and we fall prey to the GIGO (garbage in, garbage out) syndrome. What we first perceived as necessary excitements prove to be banal compared to the unique, varied, and unlimited offer that we have passed up. The final result is more boredom.

A positive and open mind is hungry for inspiring impressions that will provide grist for the mill of the active mind. The active mind needs this inspiration to transform boring moments into exciting experiences.

The mind has no problem registering millions and millions of stimuli. It has plenty of space available. Remember that the average person only uses ten percent of his brain's storage capacity!

For inspired and creative minds, quantity can never substitute quality. These minds download qualitatively, implementing factors such as educational background, personal affinities, and ambitions for the future as filters. We are the gatekeepers deciding what enters our minds. How to nurture our active minds and keep them in shape for transforming incoming inspirations into exciting ideas is the topic of the next chapter.

An Active Mind

Body fitness & Mind fitness: a Dynamic Duo

Over the last few decades, the popular Latin expression *Mens sana in corpore sana* (a healthy mind in a healthy body) has became the motto of millions of people desiring to maintain a body and soul balance in an increasingly hectic and performance-driven society. Whole industries have sprung up to meet the needs and requirements of a public looking for ways to be, or at least to feel, in great shape. Having "a sound mind in a sound body" is definitely a key element in dealing with the daily stress of 21st Century life, particularly in big cities. Millions of fitness and well-being centers all over the world offer almost 24 hour services to help us feel and look fit.

In an era in which our muscles are substituted by machines, cars, and domestic appliances, and we lead an increasing sedentary life, there is no doubt that regular physical activity benefits our body and its appearance. At the same time, however, we tend to pass our sedentary hours indulging in pre-packaged foods and beverages. The increasing demand for performance and speed in both the academic and the professional worlds gives us the emotional justification to treat ourselves to what we falsely perceive to be an "energy boost". While we obsessively go back and forth between workouts and fast-food binges to satisfy our bodily needs and cravings, we pay little attention to the fitness of our minds.

Do we go to Mind Fitness Centers? Does anyone know where they are? Shouldn't there be places that specialize in keeping minds in top condition in addition to the gymnasiums and spas that specialize in helping us to maintain our physical health? There are, fortunately, terrific centers that offer body and mind balancing activities such as Yoga and relaxation techniques. While in Western world we risk burn out in "no pain, no gain" performance environments, in some parts of the world there are cultures that have never forgotten the importance of the power of the mind in living happy, healthy, and balanced lives. The good news is that there are many wonderful places to go when we feel the need to enhance our mind fitness. The best news of all is that the most effective place is right at hand and will only cost you a small investment of your time and attention. I'm referring to your own personal mind centre, a private, upbeat and open minded institution always ready to welcome you as a frequent and active member and partner.

The mind is still active when the body sleeps

Our mind centers have a definite edge over all other body& mind centers - they never close. Open around the clock, 365 days a year, our mind centers are there for us year after year until we breathe our last breath.

The brain has a 24 clock and modern neurological research confirms that many areas of the brain function at a high level of capacity while the body rests. Scientific studies have shown that while we sleep, the brain is busy processing new information received during the day and transforming it into memory.

Since the Pre-Socratic philosophers, great thinkers have speculated about the activity of the mind during "dream time" and the ability of the human mind to prepare itself for decision-taking and problem solving while the body sleeps. "Let me sleep on it!" is a common response that springs from many millennia of human experience.

A study carried out by Sara Mednick, PhD and assistant professor of psychiatry at the University of California, San Diego, has shown that REM sleep helps us to solve problems. During the "rapid eye movement", or REM, phases of sleep, our associative networks are stimulated and our brains are able to make new and practical associations between previously unrelated stored data. According to Mednick, we can come up with solutions for old problems during our waking hours but, "for new problems, only REM sleep enhances creativity".

I can personally confirm Professor Mednick's study. My mind has sorted out millions of problems for me while I was sleeping. I would have taken many unwise decisions and lost many great opportunities in life if I hadn't learned to take the good advice to "sleep on it". One morning, after having woken up with a particularly wonderful new insight into a situation I had been turning over and over in my head for days, I wrote a poem about the wisdom of "consulting your pillow" to resolve a problem or come up with a bright, new idea. It shows that the mind –if we have a positive and active relationship with it – does not only suggest practical solutions, but also rewards us with new inspirations.

"Ask your pillow before sleeping and after awakening"

In the silence and the peace of the night

The depth of your mind becomes active and bright.

Switched off the lights of conscious, concerns, or frustrations

The depth of your mind might be blessed by divine inspirations.

(03-05-2009)

"The unconsciousness of man is the consciousness of God"

–Henry Thoreau

It is not just during the night that the unconscious mind gives us indications of what or what not to do. In his book, *Blink: The Power of Thinking without Thinking*, reporter Malcolm Gladwell writes about the split-second decision process that goes on "behind the locked door" of our minds; the ability of the mind to provide intuitive suggestions that lead us to make on-the-spot decisions in seconds. The more we train the active mind, the more it will inspire us 24 hours a day.

A fit mind: Never a boring moment

We can apply the same "use it or lose it!" body principle to the mind. Keeping the mind fit means keeping the mind active, for an active mind will reward us with many inspirations for unique creative ideas and exiting moments.

Once again, we have the good news that we don't have to make a great effort or spend a lot of money. We only have to engage the right mental gears and use the active mind in moments that we routinely consider to be "lost time". It all starts with a positive attitude and an open mind.

On the following pages are a couple of very useful, practical, and relatively easy, mind fitness techniques. I have practiced them for years and still use them today and I can guarantee-if properly and regularly done-THEY WORK!

Waiting rooms and the time you spend in them should be full of inspiration

The expression "Wait and see!" sprang from daily experience.

A traveler's life is full of waiting rooms and the long hours he or she spends in them. Picture yourself racing to the airport just to be informed at the check-in counter that your flight has been delayed several hours. It happens more often than we would like, and our first reaction is anger. Bit by bit, flight by flight, one gets used to it and learns to see the positive side of the situation. "Wow!" we tell ourselves. "Now the stress is over and I have time to read or just to relax and observe the things around me!" Waiting rooms are theatres where we can rub shoulders with other cultures, observe human behavior, watch love stories unfold, and take in fashion shows. Even the most open mind has to work overtime to register all interesting things that deserve its attention.

Depending on your mood at the moment, you can pick and choose what to observe. Perhaps the elderly couple facing you, surrounded by plastic bags bearing toyshop logos, attracts your attention. A big toy truck is sticking out of one of the bags. Another one seems to be full of things for a newborn baby.

The couple seems to be rather nervous about the delay, constantly looking up at the information screen and then glancing down at their watches. Every fifteen minutes, the woman gets up and asks another traveler if they are at the right gate for the flight to Toronto. After receiving an affirmative and reassuring answer, she turns back to her husband who is waiting anxiously for her update. His face relaxes with the assurance that they are in the right place, and he tenderly takes her hand as she sits down beside him.

Your curiosity aroused, your eyes zoom in on them like a hawk's. You notice that the husband's brown sandals are worn and that his grey wool socks have been mended over and over. Your mind creates a narrative about these strangers that is better than any Hollywood movie. They are going to visit their son or daughter who lives in Canada. They are not used to travelling. They are not very wealthy and they have saved up over time to make this dream happen. It is one of the most exciting trips of their life because they will spend precious time with their grandchildren. Taking another quick scan at the shopping bags you decide that one of the grandchildren must be a three- or four- year-old boy and the other a baby girl. You picture their arrival and welcome at the airport in Toronto in your mind: tears of happiness, hugs all around, a reunion of three generations.

This might be just one of the endless wonderful stories you could discover in an airport or a railway station, at a bus stop, or in the reception area of your doctor's or lawyer's office - not to mention those other lines we wait in to vote, buy lottery tickets, or pay for our groceries. If we could calculate the percentage of our lives we spend waiting, we would be astonished at the number of hours it represented.

For a positive, open, and active mind, these places and the time we spend in them can be golden opportunities to observe and think; living theatres full of anecdotes and narratives that can amuse and inspire us. The next time you find yourself in a waiting room, pull out a piece of paper and jot down some notes on what you see around you. Transform the time "lost" waiting into a moment for indulging your whimsy and creativity.

Empty Rooms can be full of details

"That's fine," you might say. "It's easy to get inspired where there are interesting things that grab your attention but what about those horrible, boring, completely sterile, empty, and silent places such as hospital corridors, prisons, army barracks, or budget motel rooms? How am I going to feel uplifted and creative between four walls whose paint is so faded that no one could tell me what the original color might have been, or in a place so silent that I only have my own breath to keep me company?

I am not going to be ridiculous and claim that empty and silent places are as interesting and stimulating as the other settings I have previously described, but they might not really be as dull as they appear at first sight. Imagine yourself alone in an empty and silent warehouse or an old airplane hangar. After a few minutes you begin to relax. There is no noise clamoring in your ears. How wonderful it is to enjoy a few minutes of silence! You begin to really listen, and after a short interval, you hear a constant regular sound and identify it as something dripping. You follow the sound, drip by drop, until you locate a corner where a small puddle is forming on the floor. You start noticing the many different faded colors of the rusty pipes that line the walls, below ceilings mottled by humidity and the microscopic filtration of water. Your senses start sending messages to the brain that immediately sends back requests for more data. You smell the odor of the past that seems to seep out of the walls and the wooden beams that surround you. You hear a cooing and a flapping of wings from the rafters above you and discover that you are not alone.

The American composer John Cage once wrote a "silent" concert piece for piano, hoping to inspire audiences to listen more intently to the world around them and find beauty in what at first might seem to them to be a total absence of sound. The hand-written musical score of this work, titled *4' 33"*, did not contain any musical notations at all, except for divisions between its three movements that together lasted four minutes and thirty-three seconds. Premiered in an open air summer theatre, 4' 33" surprised and outraged most concert goers present, but the few people willing to accept Cage's invitation to listen with a open mind described the first movement as filled with the sound of wind in the surrounding trees and the second movement as pulsating with the rhythm of raindrops! We wouldn't want every concert we attended to be like 4' 33", but we can be inspired by it to use our creativity to perceive and appreciate the subtle and unexpected music of quiet places.

Some of the greatest works of literature, history, religion, and philosophy were written in the silence of the bleakest, least inspiring, place in the world: a prison cell. The cultural heritage these works comprise is compelling proof that an active mind can draw from its vast warehouse of references and find inspiration where a bored and frustrated mind would be driven to desperation. Saint Paul wrote his letters to the Ephesians, Philippians, Colossians, and Philemon while incarcerated for teaching the Gospel, and Miguel Cervantes wrote the classic *Don Quixote* in a debtor's prison. French historian Fernand Braudel wrote the first draft of *The Mediterranean and the Mediterranean World in the Age of Philip II*, one of the scholarly masterpieces of the 20th century, in a German prisoner-of-war camp with virtually no reference books to prompt his memory. If we include the writings of Gandhi and Martin Luther King's famous "Letter from a Birmingham Jail" to this list, it might inspire us to consider the time we spend stuck waiting for the bus or in line at the post office as time "freed up" from other responsibilities to meditate, dream, or observe life around us. These are perfect moments to remember a funny joke, imagine ourselves on a Caribbean beach, or close our eyes and relive a passionate kiss.

One little detail can stimulate and amuse you in a moment of boredom

An active mind is always curious and never gets bored sorting through the interesting things the open mind has detected. It's a question of developing the right attitude and a habit of studying and creatively interpreting what we find around us for our own amusement. This is the surest way of living more exciting moments than boring ones. The more you use your mind, the more skilled it will become in informing, entertaining, and inspiring you. "Use it or lose it!" Here is a simple technique that will work like vitamin supplement for your mind:

Pick a moment during the day or night when your mind is not occupied and open a dialogue with it. Just let your senses wander freely until they alert you to something interesting around you. It doesn't really matter which senses are activated. It's only important that one or more of them identifies one extraordinary detail of a completely ordinary thing. What appear to be the most unimportant things can be amazingly interesting if you take the empty room approach mentioned earlier. Your sensory reverie could be triggered by something as simple as running your fingers through your hair. Pulling your hand away, you notice that a stray hair has fallen in your lap. Your sense of sight initiates a process of observation and your sense of touch enters into the game. The stray hair you are observing is one of the hundreds of thousands of hairs growing on your body. Each one carries your unique genetic code. A simple mental exercise like this can expand in a million directions. It's possible that a similar observation inspired O. Henry to write his classic Christmas story "A Gift of the Magi". Did a beautiful, long shank of brown hair seen by the author in a shop window inspire him to create the character of Della, the loving wife who sold her long tresses for the money to buy her husband Jim a Christmas present? Think of all the crimes that have been solved by the discovery of a single hair or the song lyrics dedicated to the subject. If the stray hair is grey, the mind will be stimulated by the options: go platinum or call the hair salon tomorrow?

One sentence can fill a book

An active mind has a high associational capacity and just a few words can lead it to enough exciting reflections about a topic to fill a book. A vivid example is one of phrases that inspired this book: "As usual!" One day, I heard a bored-looking person answer the question "How is everything today?" with **"As usual!"** muttered in a bored tone of voice and it instantly struck me that people routinely repeat these phrases like the recorded messages of answering machines.

I asked myself why we tend to repeat the same old boring questions and answers. I observed that too many people walk through life like extras through a movie set, repeating the same scene over and over again, every time in exactly the same way. What would it take for us to be protagonists with ever changing roles in our own exciting life movies instead of anonymous, bored, and boring extras with only walk-on roles in a standardized working and living environment that offers us no satisfaction or personal creative outlet? For an active mind, one question or one answer can develop into a complete story that crosses professional, cultural, and national borders and creates new and exciting personal horizons.

The active mind loves every detail of practically EVERYTHING that sparks the thought process, knowing that, in most cases, the reward of thinking is enjoying many stimulating moments.

An active mind falls in love with nature

Human beings have an ancestral relation with nature. We are a natural part of its vast and fascinating tapestry. As an American-Indian proverb says: "We are made from Mother Earth and we go back to Mother Earth."

If we were to research which themes have been the most inspiring for artists throughout history, we would quickly realize there are two. They are love and nature. We shouldn't be surprised. It's completely natural! They provide the warp and woof of the fabric of our lives, the history of our planet, and that of the universe.

Thank God we are not resistant to the appeal of the diverse and unlimited beauty of nature. We instinctively call it Mother. We respond to its enchantments and fall in love with it. With a positive mind, open, and active mind, our senses enter into a state of ecstasy when we contemplate nature in its purest state. Our sensorial orchestra plays a harmonious symphony of our love for nature, full of birdsong and sounds of leaves rustling in the evening breeze.

Immersed in nature, the mind activates, opens, and becomes more positive. There is no doubt that a conscious, trained, and active mind gets more out of it.

There is simply no higher source of inspiration than nature, with its diversity, immensity, and fascinating microscopic details. Watching a butterfly landing on a beckoning flower, who doesn't feel the urge to spread his wings too?

There is no better place to dream about beauty, love, or peace than in the heart of the nature. Unspoiled nature is a place to dream. German poet Victor Blüthgen wrote, **"If you have dreaming eyes the world is full of magic!"** Imagine the magic of the full glory of nature. It makes a lot of sense to remember what we've read about how animals use their senses in their natural habitats. Take a bird's eye view and admire the amazing landscapes before you: there is not one exactly the same as another in the entire world. Each one is unique. Even if you are used to gazing at the same landscape every day, look at it again from a different angle and you will discover new elements. This technique is not only useful for contemplating landscapes and other material objects. It can also be applied to how you look at your inner mindscapes. Are you bored with the same old images that always spring to mind? Is there something wrong with the mental picture that you would like to improve? You can change the way you view your personal mental landscapes and that changed vision will help you to improve what you see. Look at the problem or opportunity in question through the lens of an active mind. Now zoom with your eyes to just one little detail, such as a leaf, and you will discover how its delicate nerves trace a wonderful design pulsing with life. Closely inspect a problem or an opportunity through the lens of your active mind and the details you see will lead you to better inspirations and sounder decisions.

One day I was walking along one of my favorite country trails. I love to take my time on this particular route without rushing, just to see things I have never noticed before. On that particular day, I discovered an impressive fig tree I had never given any attention to before. I was captivated by the overall attractiveness of the tree, and in particular, by the beauty of its beautiful, big leaves. Fig leaves are very lovely. When Eve had to cover part of her body after she bit into the forbidden apple, she used a fig leaf. Was it a coincidence? I don't think so. The size and the beauty of the fig leaf must have made it the world's first fashion sensation. I took one of the leaves in my hand and was impressed by the perfection of the design. I reached for another and scanned the details of its design. The pattern created by the central rib and the veins branching out of it made the leaf look like a little piece of green cloth with a perfect little tree embroidered on it, a design appealing enough to be the inspiration for an entire fashion collection. Then I compared the first with the second and realized that they were not exactly the same; that there were fine differences in all the details. It was a perfect illustration of how each molecule of everything that exists is unique. Just like a human being, every leaf has its own way of expressing itself and its own unique life, its own DNA.

"It's all the same!" is the perception of a bored mind, the mind that does not register or sufficiently appreciate the little but important differences.

What looks the same at first glance is not the same to a trained eye. A shepherd can see the distinguishing marks that make each of his sheep unique; differences that an outsider might never be able to distinguish. My lesson learned from country walks is that a little focused observation can be the wellspring of many exciting narratives created by an active mind. Observe, interpret, and create is exactly what an active mind does.

Can you imagine the millions of little stories we can create, live, and share, every moment and every day? Each lived moment is unique and will never be repeated. It is unique to our lifetime and all of eternity and should, by definition, not be boring. The decision is ours to make as to whether the moments we live are exciting and worth registering in our memory.

The active mind interprets what the open mind detects. The active mind makes up stories, composes, paints, and turns impulses into tangible manifestations of ideas. These are exciting moments for immediate, delightful, consumption or to be stored away as differed pleasures.

Nature is THE source of inspiration and exciting feelings and moments. He who is bored by nature has lost an invaluable part of his own being. Whenever you have an inspired moment, try jotting down a few words on a piece of paper to reflect upon later. **Jot it down and POST it** and you'll never be bored or lose a memorable moment you have lived.

Jot it down and POST IT!

More than once, a spontaneous idea may have flashed through your mind and you have thought, "That's interesting. I have to remember that as it's worth following up." A little while later, when you try to come back to it, it has unfortunately faded from your memory, although neither your age nor your mental capacity can justify the forgetfulness. It's something that happens to all of us. Spontaneous inspirations are falling stars that you need to catch and put in your pocket or, in an instant, they fade away, often forever. I used to get very upset when I lost an inspiration this way, because losing an inspiration implied losing a great idea or a golden opportunity to do something interesting. Then I made a decision to always carry with me the simplest and most instantly accessible memory tools: paper and ink.

Papyrus & Ink: the skin and blood of an active mind

The Chinese made what was perhaps the first ink out of soot, lamp oil thickened with gelatin from animal skins, and musk, around 5000 BC and the Egyptians developed papyrus as a writing support from the papyrus plants growing along the banks of the Nile River circa 3000 BC. Since these discoveries, human beings have come to depend on the written document and have made it the principle means of documenting their lives. Thanks to these ancient techniques, we enjoy a rich legacy of historical documents that testify to our past and inform our future.

The digitalization of the world changed the role of paper and ink. I use my computer to do many things. My laptop is an excellent 21st century assistant for writing and filing documents, images and sounds. I appreciate everything it can do, but I can't imagine living without that 21st century papyrus, paper, or its inseparable liquid companion, ink. For me, they are the skin and the blood of an active mind.

The company that developed and introduced those little "sticky notes" might have done it only for commercial reasons, but they had a truly great idea. Today, billions of little memory-prompting stickers can be found on almost any type of surface to remind somebody to do something or just to record something that simply should not be forgotten.

Jotting things down and posting them is one of the greatest habits of an active mind. You if have no other place to post your inspirations and observations when they come flying at you, jot them down on sticky notes and post them on your body. Your new "second skin" will clothe you in inspiration. When a creative person has a brilliant idea, he writes it down on whatever surface is available: coffee shop napkins, shirt cuffs – even the back of his hand.

I do this and more than once I've had to scrub the note off with soap and water after the idea was safely transferred to my computer. Some people swear by their small digital notebooks. If they serve the purpose, why not use them? I, myself, continue to prefer the sensual experience of putting pen to paper and later reviewing what I've written in my own unique handwriting.

Zero communication, zero excitement

Human beings cannot live without communicating with the world around them. It is known that a baby bereft of human warmth, physical contact, and heartwarming words will be seriously affected and may even get sick. It is not any different with old people. A lack of attention and opportunity to communicate with others can deteriorate their health and accelerate the aging process. In fact everyone, regardless of his or her age, needs to communicate to live a happy and healthy life.

Once someone, who most probably wanted to impress me with the perfect relationship he supposedly enjoyed with his wife of over twenty years, proudly told me that during their long relationship there had never been friction between them. I couldn't resist asking him, with a sense of humor, of course, if the lack of friction came from a lack of contact. The chagrined expression on his face left no doubt that he had fallen in his own trap of overstatement and that my innocent teasing had revealed an uncomfortable truth.

It's no secret that without contact there is no communication, positive or negative. A simple caress, a sympathetic glance, or a kind word can be as positive for the person bestowing it as it is for its recipient. It makes us feel good to be a part of a communicating and interacting world.

Much has been written on the subject of communication. I love this quote by author, columnist, and life coach Martha Beck about the importance of human contact: "Basic human contact - the meeting of eyes, the exchanging of words - is to the psyche what oxygen is to the brain. If you're feeling abandoned by the world, interact with anyone you can." A life without communication is by definition unnatural, lonely, and boring.

In our daily lives we make contact with many people that we might consider less than exiting, or sometimes outright boring, but if we shy away from contact, we will lose our talent for communication and whatever possibility we might have had to establish more exiting encounters and relationships in the future.

In our fast paced society we have a tendency to think that we do not have sufficient time to communicate personally. Since we've got a wide range of digital options, we convince ourselves that a smiley face tacked onto an email is an adequate substitute for our voice or our presence. It's wonderful that we can digitalize everything from birthday wishes to our legal signature, but an electronic pulse is no substitute for eye to eye contact, a firm handshake, or a warm embrace.

The more people work together as a team and are expected to be effective and happy on the job, the more important personal, direct, and tangible communication becomes, and the more important it is for managers to resist the temptation to rely exclusively upon digital communications. In his book *It's Your Ship*, an interesting exposé of management techniques utilized on a ship that became a benchmark for quality and efficiency in the U.S. Navy, Captain D. Michael Abrashoff states the following: "Social interaction is getting lost in a digital world that trades more in abstractions than in face to face relations. It's more than a shame-it's a bottom line mistake."

What happens when two people meet depends completely upon their attitude, the chemistry between them, and above all, their emotional ability to establish positive contact. Having a positive, open, and active mind is the key to creating mutually beneficial communications. It is one of the ABC's of emotional intelligence. Even those who are neither born nor trained communicators can do a lot to avoid being a communications ZERO and suffering a boring life of missed opportunities. Let's go through a couple of simple examples.

Imagine that you have to solve some problems related to official documents and you find yourself queuing up in a huge, drab, and overcrowded government office. When after a long wait it is finally your turn, you're in a bad mood for having lost so much time in a boring place. The civil servant who now faces you might also be bored after hours and hours at his routine job in a boring place and stressed-out by the constant stream of negative comments and complaints of the people he attends. What can you expect from this situation? Eventually, the required documents will get signed, stamped, and registered, or you will be referred to another office where you can resolve your problem. It would be a shame, however, not to make the encounter at least a little bit more pleasant for both you and the civil servant before you. Never lose the chance to transform "negative vibrations" into positive experiences. When we are bored, angry, and frustrated we often forget to ask important questions or we don't hear useful advice. If you manage to exchange just a few pleasantries instead of snarling at each other, it's a big breakthrough in human communications and you'll feel better for the experience.

There is a simple way to deal with almost any type of situation and to almost always get quicker and better results. It's called communication through human contact. A positive, open, and active mind can make your day and someone else's too. Bring a positive and open mindset to all your encounters. Your facial expression and the tone of your voice will communicate your positive attitude in seconds to the other person and dispose him or her to be friendlier and to treat you well.

An immediate and natural chemistry between people is a big boon in first encounters, but we can't always count on it. Although not everyone creates the same instant empathy, a positive attitude transmitted via direct eye contact, a warm greeting, or a friendly handshake is always a good opener. Not looking into the eyes of the person you are addressing is the equivalent of not talking to him. A simple word like "Hello!" can be sufficient to open a conversation with a new person, but it depends a lot on how you say it. Using an inappropriate tone of voice when making initial contact with someone can create a communication barrier difficult to overcome later, no matter what we do. There is a French saying that puts it very precisely: *C,est le ton qui fait la musique* (It's the tone that makes the music). If we want our words to be music to another's ears, we should always remember that the tone of our voices can make the decisive difference. People are generally sensitive enough to pick up on your tone of voice in microseconds and will react and respond according to the initial impression you have left in the minds.

Few people on Earth are completely insensitive to human contact. If you can create a minimal spark in your initial contact with someone, the opportunity for good communication and an interesting encounter is there for you.

Let's look at another scenario in which a brief chance encounter turns out to be fortuitous.

> One day you happen to be trapped in rush hour traffic while driving to an important doctor's appointment. You've been waiting for weeks for this appointment as this particular specialist is very much in demand. You look at your watch and discover that you risk arriving too late at your destination. Although every second counts, you make an exception to the road warrior behavior all around you and take pity on a woman who needs to enter your lane of traffic to make a left turn. Making eye contact with her, you indicate with a smile and hand signal that you are giving her the opportunity to change lanes. You register her expression of gratitude before she disappears from view. When you finally arrive at the doctor's office, your watch tells you that you've already blown the appointment, but you enter with a smile anyway. The first face that greets you confirms that it's a small world after all: The doctor's assistant at the reception desk is the lady you made space for in the rush hour traffic on the way and she recognizes you in seconds. To make a long story short: You are treated like a VIP and conversing with her, you even discover that she is the wife of an important superior in your company's headquarters! **An amazing story, but these things can really happen.**

One simple, well made initial contact can lead to incredible scenarios in which you can be the main protagonist. For many people, just ONE great contact was a determining factor in their lives.

Take the challenge to engage in one in-depth reflection every day

An active mind loves to be challenged, because a good challenge keeps the mind fit. An excellent daily challenge for our active mind is to give our undivided attention to something new we've seen every day and engage in an in-depth reflection about it. The object of our attention is not that important. Whatever it is, it is bound to have some aspect worthy of our concentrated attention that will ignite our curiosity and lead us on to more profound questions and answers. Don't forget to jot them down and post them!

Imagine that by chance you notice a rusty old soda can in an otherwise clean street. It doesn't make a lot of sense to you until you observe a poorly dressed, elderly man carrying a clear plastic bag full of old cans fifty meters away... O.K. This time I'm not going to complete the exercise for you. Give it a try. From the bit of information given above, your mind could weave the story of an entire life.

I personally started doing this type of mind challenge based on conscious observations many years ago and many times the exercise has given me great ideas that I wrote down and later developed into interesting and exciting projects.

A very inspiring way to act on our impulses using our open mind, our heightened senses, and our immediate reflections and feelings is composing an aphorism or a short poem. Writing poems, proverbs, maxims, or aphorisms is a top mind stimulator, as it involves combining linguistic skills with creative inspiration and balancing both rational and emotional content. It is also an excellent training tool for sharpening the skills one needs to dialogue and to convince others. Everyone, however, has a way of expressing what they have gleaned from their daily reflection. For people with musical talent, their daily reflection might be the inspiration for a new composition. For visual artists, a new painting, sculpture, illustration, or photograph might be the result. For the technologically or scientifically oriented nature, a daily reflection might lead to new insights into how to deal with a particular aspect of a search for new solutions, or the discovery of new questions worth being answered.

Just ONE deeper reflection per day about ONE little aspect of something–preferably not related to our normal usual jobs or preoccupations–can be a very gratifying use of a few minutes of our time because it will lead to new, exciting, moments and experiences. The idea that you don't have the time to do it is no excuse. A 24 hour day is made up of 1,440 minutes. Surely we can dedicate a few of them to benefitting our active mind and planting the seeds of more excitement and satisfaction in our lives.

Live at least 150 years

Life is very short and the natural process of aging and the fast pace of modern life make it seem even shorter. Who hasn't heard comments about how swiftly the years seem to fly by like, "I don't understand it, but the last ten years have flown by like a blip on the radar screen of eternity. Where has the time gone?"

When considered in the context of eternity, our life span becomes immeasurable and incomprehensible in terms of human understanding. If *one's* life in the *span* of *eternity* is but a *breath,* as the psalmists tell us, we should focus on taking long, deep, breaths and live every moment to the fullest.

The American poet and philosopher Henry David Thoreau (1817-1862) wrote the following about eternity:

> **"You must live in the present, launch yourself on every wave, and find your eternity in each moment."**

This is clear advice to live life, love life, be grateful for each moment we are alive, and try to experience the moments we are given as waves of excitement.

 The average lifespan in the developed world is between 75 and 80 years. Only a few centuries ago it was less than half that number. Through science, we might one day discover the yet-to-be-decoded physical or biological secrets that will lead to a considerably extended human longevity. Some futurists believe that with the tremendous scientific and technological progress we have at hand, we might soon extend longevity up to 125 years. According to some prophets of the future, nanorobots introduced into our bodies, in combination with sophisticated diet supplements, will eventually be able to ward off diseases and arrest our physical deterioration.

Having a positive and open mind I welcome this vision, but my active mind tells me not to put too much faith in it in the short and midterm. My active mind advises me to make the best of my life here and now, cherishing each moment with an intense consciousness, and above all, trying to feel happy. An interesting article in the New York Times of July 15, 2009, "Long life is all about a state of mind", by columnist Roger Cohen, explores the importance of happiness in our lives and its implications in helping us to live longer. In this article Cohen shares a family experience that deserves mentioning here in the context of what we are discussing: "My mother died of cancer at 69. Her father lived to 98, her mother to 104. I said my mother died of cancer. But that's not true. She was bipolar and depression devastated her. What took her life was misery."

We are well advised to cultivate healthy living habits and to strive to maintain a high perceived level of life enjoyment–a positive psychological state of mind that reflects one's ability to interact pleasurably with one's environment. People who manifest a high perceived level of life enjoyment live more intensely than those who have a low perception of their level of enjoyment in life. Feeling intensely alive and happy means accumulating more of those exiting moments I've been talking so much about. **If we double our perceived level of life enjoyment by making the most of every moment, it's like living out the joy of two lifetimes**. In this way, we can consider that we are doubling the average 75 year life expectancy and making 150 years out of it. Living a healthy and happy century and a half is three times more than our forefathers lived just 150 years ago. One hundred fifty years of intense enjoyment and wellbeing registered on our Hard & Heart disks is not a bad deal.

Time is money but, more importantly, time is life

The expression "time is money" was coined in the United States by Benjamin Franklin, whose advice to a young businessman was: **"Remember that Time is Money!"**

It is very true that time can be measured in monetary terms. But whereas time is not a synonym for money, it is a synonym for life. **Time is Life.** Life is measured by seconds, hours, and years. The sundial reminds us

Tempus fugit (Latin, Time flies). With every second that passes, our life becomes shorter and we can never turn back to capture the lost moments. Time should be a measure of our quality of life, our personal perception of feeling good about ourselves and our lives. Every second is worth living, and living well. Every second, minute, hour, day, and year counts in our endeavor to feel healthy, loved, and know joy of living. A happy and fulfilled life is the sum of every moment lived to the fullest. A life lived to the fullest might have different meaning for each individual. The popular Spanish toast *Salud! Amor! y Dinero!* (Health, Love, and Money!) does a good job of prioritizing these three things that we all desire. Money can help to make life easier, but there are many real life stories that prove that even with all the money of the world, we can find ourselves with a low ranking on the quality of life scale, perhaps for lack of time or the wisdom to enjoy what we have. One thing is unquestionable: a boring life lacks excitement and without exciting moments there is no quality of life.

A morning candy and an evening sweetie

The greatest positivists amongst us cannot avoid the fact that in a 24 hour day NOT every moment is going to be sweet. Some of them can be even quite bitter. That's a good reason to **try to treat ourselves to just one little sweetie every morning and every night.** A sweet incentive in the morning prepares us for the rest of the day with its real life opportunities and challenges and a tasty treat in the evening is a nice final touch. The first and most important one is, of course, the morning candy, to put us in a good morning mood and energize our minds at least until lunchtime.

What is "Morning Candy"?

Imagine opening your eyes in the morning, slowly shaking off your drowsiness, and suddenly having an inspiration or an interesting thought come to you. You reach out for it and grasp it, and turning it over in your mind, it becomes a great and useful idea for your workday or a moment of leisure time later on. When this sort of thing happens the first thing in the morning it makes you feel good. That's "morning candy". An active mind will frequently give you an inspiration in your first waking moments. Use it to make more of the day ahead.

Picture yourself waking up and becoming aware of your own breathing. You are alive and so is the day. The morning light that peeps through the closed blinds tells you so. You open the curtains and regard the world outside.

Even if the day isn't sunny, you enjoy the rain, the wind, or the snow because they are all vital signals of a living world you are part of. Your morning reflections should always include forming a positive outlook towards the weather.

You take a nice hot shower and feel the water massaging your skin. Your soft towel gives you a second massage. That's all morning candy. You inhale the fragrances of the soap, aftershave, body lotion, and perfume that fill the air and you feel good. "How wonderful it is to have all this", you think gratefully. That's morning candy too. Taking a little time to choose which dress, tie, or T shirt you'd like to wear that day can be a form of morning candy.

Breakfast is, perhaps, the most obvious morning candy, whether it is coffee or tea, toast and jam, or a fresh apple. A little exercise to warm up your muscles, or a short walk or jog by yourself with your dog, can also be morning candy because you enjoy what you're doing and your body and soul feel gratified.

If you wake up to somebody you love and appreciate, reward their presence with a kiss, a smile, and a nice word or grateful glance. Don't forget the dog and the parakeet. They need their morning candy too! What all morning candies have in common is the ability to sweeten up your day right from the start and give you the positive energy boost you need to start the day with inspiration.

What is "The Evening Sweetie?"

If taking your morning candy has helped you to see the sweeter side of life during the day, it's also possible that you might have had a few unavoidable bitter moments too. If you arrive home after a day that has left a bitter taste in your mouth, you are well-advised to treat yourself to an "evening sweetie". Even if your day has gone well, and you are still savoring the morning candy, there is always room for a bit more sweetness in your life.

We all have a long list of must-do chores at home, but it is important to balance our responsibilities with rewards for having done our best all day. You might just want to relax and listen to your favorite music, prepare something special in the kitchen, cuddle up on the couch with a loved one, or take a long, luxurious bath. They are all good candidates for being your evening sweetie. You could take a walk around the corner, go to the gym, attend an evening class or lecture, or play with your kids. The evening is a good time to pay attention to the pets that have been waiting patiently for you all day long or commune with your houseplants. Whatever you do, get inspired to make evening sweeties out of every evening activity. Evening hours are precious hours to feel truly alive and happy before the day is over.

There are as many evening sweeties as there are individual tastes, but each and every one should charge your active mind with positive energy and inspiration. Your evening sweeties will help you to sleep better and wake up in a good frame of mind for contemplating the next morning candy. You can share your unique inspirations for morning candy and evening sweetie recipes with others seeking to turn routine and boredom into more joy of living through the website **www.proexcitingmoments.com**

Escape from "The Usual" Spread your wings!

We were born with wings

Human beings have always been inspired by flight. Since time immemorial, we have gazed at the skies inspired by the soaring of birds and the more humble trajectory of insects. In our wakeful daydreams and our unconscious dreams at night, we spread our imaginary wings and cease to be earthbound.

The many psychological reasons for this deeply rooted behavior, studied and written about by philosophers and psychologists, are beyond the scope of this book, but one fact is clear: we all have an innate wanderlust. The constant desire to embark on both physical and mental journeys is common to all cultures.

Travel has unquestionable benefits. It enriches our minds through practical experience and provides us with new, exciting, and inspiring moments shared with other cultures. Sometimes travel even brings us face to face with people of socio-economic classes that we seldom mix with at home. If I could make an addition to the list of internationally recognized human rights, it would be the right to travel, although I know that this is a utopian idea considering there are hundreds of millions of people in the world still fighting for their most basic rights.

History is full of great travelers who have lived the excitement of travelling.

Millions of our ancestors were seasoned travelers who set out on epic migrations with only what they could carry on their backs. Many of these voyagers were forced to travel by climatic changes in their home territories, or driven by hunger, sought better hunting grounds.

In more recent times, however, many travelers have left home out of curiosity to learn and the urge to explore places unknown to them. Our history and science books tell us about many pioneering travelers who brought back new insights and ideas from their voyages that changed our frontiers, attitudes, behaviors, and even our diets. These journeys of exploration also left their mark on the lands and cultures discovered. Great damage was often done for the greater glory of kings, and even in the name of God.

It is far beyond the scope of this book to mention all the courageous and inspired travelers who broadened our horizons, but two deserve special mention for being paradigms in the history of travel: Marco Polo and Ibn Battuta.

The first is the most popular and most well-known, particularly in the Western world, but the second travelled 75,000 miles more than the other. Most importantly, their very different cultural backgrounds and personalities made them different kinds of travelers who left distinct legacies behind them.

Marco Polo, who lived from1254 to 1324, was certainly more expert in marketing his own exploits, as can be witnessed by the many travel-related institutions or companies that bear his name today. Born into a prosperous

Venetian merchant family, he followed his father's footsteps in the trade of goods between Asia and the West. Many of the Asian goods and customs that now are a part of Western culture were originally introduced by Marco Polo.

Ibn Battuta was born in Fez, Morocco, in 1304. It was there that he received his spiritual and scientific education. His first trip abroad was a pilgrimage to the holy city of Mecca. From there he continued travelling, crossing countries and continents for 29 long years.

He dove deep into all the cultures he encountered; learning, teaching, marrying, and even serving as a royal advisor and judge. He learned to speak several languages and is known for being one of the first multicultural scholars. Like Marco Polo, he had an open mind– a precondition for learning from, and adapting to, other cultures.

Both of these travelers introduced to their native cultures information and ideas that are still relevant today. Whenever you set out from home, travel with the open mind, courage, and passion for adventure that characterized Marco Polo and Ibn Battuta. If you do so, you'll be rewarded with experiences and memories that you will treasure your whole life through.

Crossing borders is learning new limits

When we were kids, my father told us the story of his first voyage over and over again, always with the same glow in his eyes and the same pleasure in reliving the tale. His first journey was a coming-of-age celebration. He had dreamed since childhood of biking from his little village in the Netherlands to the harbor town of Antwerp, in Belgium. Now a fully-grown 18 year old, he could make his dream of adventure come true.

The distance between his village and Antwerp was only 120 kilometers, but in those days, when few people travelled far from home, it was thought to be considerable. Undaunted by the road ahead, early one sunny summer morning my father rolled out of town astride a shiny new bike. This bicycle seemed to fly through the familiar lowlands and his mood soared with it. How good it was to be as free as a bird and have nothing in the way of his dreams and ambitions! Nothing in the way at all, until he reached the

Belgian frontier, that when my father was young, long before the European Union put an end to checkpoints between European countries, was still a real border with frontier police and barriers.

 The police stopped him and asked to see his passport. New as he was to the world of foreign travel, he had not been aware that he needed a passport. Who in his village had ever had a passport? In that moment, my father realized for the first time that facing a new frontier could also mean facing one's limits. That meant time limits as well, as it was now too late to turn back home. He spent the night in what he always good naturedly referred to as a little border hotel (in truth, the border holding cell for prisoners) and was sent back home the next morning without further punishment. Later on in life, he would visit Antwerp on various occasions, but by that time, his vehicle had four wheels and an engine and he went well equipped with a valid passport.

 History has a habit of repeating itself. Approximately 35 years later, when I was 16, I had the same dream of setting out on my bicycle from the same little village in Netherlands, but my chosen destination was Paris. The distance was 520 kilometers, almost four times my father's own ambitious goal. He defended my plans in front of my mother and bought two new bikes – one for me and one for my 14 year old brother, who had lost no time in signing on to the expedition.

Although more skeptical than my father about the planned adventure, my mother equipped us with a tent and cooking utensils that included a little gas cooker to warm up the instant soup she had packed for us to eat in the evening before setting up camp for the night. As accumulated human experience gets handed down from one generation to another, we set out with a good set of maps and valid passports.

We pedaled out of the village on a fine early summer morning with high spirits, just as my father had done many years before, once again sailing southward through the broad, flat landscape with no more than a minimal physical effort. Everything was great until the flatland ended and we began to pedal our way up a series of soft, rolling hills. The pressure on our legs seemed overwhelming as we bravely pushed our bikes forward. We were accustomed to the flat, open landscape of the Netherlands and these gentle hills seemed like mountain peaks to us. We set up our tent early that day and slept like two logs until a curious cow stuck her head into our tent and woke us up in the morning.

After a quick breakfast we were back on the route. The hills seemed to go on forever. Every time we reached the top of one, drenched in sweat and dying of thirst, we gleaned the horizon in hope of finding flatlands ahead. The hills continued and the road signs indicated that we still had hundreds of kilometers yet to go. Late that afternoon, trying to pedal up yet another hill, my brother nearly collapsed from exhaustion and we called it quits early for the second day in a row. My brother broke down and cried a bit. Feeling guilty, I took care of him the best that I could. We were learning an important lesson: Crossing borders means discovering new and challenging situations that push you to new limits. But it can be worth pushing those limits and discovering new and wider personal frontiers.

The next day at high noon we pedaled through the heart of Paris, and when we passed the world famous Arch of Triumph, our own sense of personal triumph swelled our hearts.

One day, my own kids may cross new borders many kilometers farther away than the distance between my hometown and Paris. Perhaps it will be an opportunity for them to test their limits and assume new challenges, just as it was for my brother and me. This is what travelling is really about, and I'll be happy and proud if they continue this family tradition.

Know which limits not to cross

A positive, open, and active mind can be a gateway to exciting travel experiences. However, there are a few things we need to understand if we don't want our hosts to roll up the welcome mat and close their hearts to us.

The three criteria for a traveler should always be: **Respect! Respect! Respect!**

That may seem to be no more than simple common sense, but without realizing it, we often leave our common sense at home when we travel to foreign lands.

One well-known trap that any traveler can easily fall into is making the wrong comment to a self-deprecating host. This is a hard trap to spot because your very own cultural sensitivity might seduce you to cross invisible cultural limits.

People who have a broad education and have travelled a good deal are well aware that there are sociological and cultural differences between them and their foreign hosts. These differences can even crop up in conversations between people who have every intention to be courteous and respectful and who might even have many things in common. It is perfectly natural that people you meet while travelling in foreign countries will try to draw you out on certain topics to discover what your opinion of, and attitude towards, their country really is.

One classic tactic of revealing your pre-conceived notions and prejudices is self-criticism on the part of your hosts. It most commonly takes the form of making self-deprecating comments or criticisms of the host's culture. If someone starts doing this, don't bite the hook. These self-criticisms are often repetitions of clichés this person has endured since childhood about his or her culture. If someone tells you, "We are a bit unorganized," he is probably not expressing his own opinion but, instead, repeating the foreign perception of his society as a chaotic, undisciplined, tribe with no sense of collective responsibility just to see how you'll react. As all cultures have their stereotypes, your host's offhand remark could also reflect the other extreme: "We are a bit overly organized," a self-criticism rife with fears of being perceived as one-dimensional, inflexible, boring, or uncreative. Be careful! These passing comments are traps set to test your mindset and your attitude towards the host culture.

Anyone who has ever entered into a conversation has hoped that the other person would bring out the best in him. Any person who has ever really wanted to communicate with a stranger has sought to diminish mutual negative perceptions and has striven to find positive things the two had in common. People in the countries you visit want you to respect the differences between your culture and theirs. You may think your own culture is better than any other, but don't let your pride in your own culture make you small-minded or arrogant. No place in the world is perfect, and presenting oneself as Mr. or Mrs. Perfection is not a good tactic if one would like to have a sincere and whole-hearted welcome.

Everyone likes to have an outsider's confirmation of what makes them proud, whether it's their personal achievements, their religion, their country, their vegetable garden or their grandchildren. It makes sense to learn what topics to pursue and what topics to avoid when travelling outside of your own country. The more a discussion approaches political matters and religious beliefs, the more respectful and careful we should be. Observe, learn, listen, and be cautious and respectful.

There are two fool-proof ways of making friends anywhere in the world: compliment your host or your waiter on the food you've been served, and show an interest in the local soccer, cricket, or baseball team. Interest in the local team or compliments to the chef will almost always result in an invitation to share a table, a recipe, or a story. In my opinion, a place at the table in a foreign country is a cherished opportunity to feel the intimate pulse of that culture. If you are invited to share a table with a native of your host country, and show the proper gratitude for the gesture of hospitality he or she has shown, you will have almost guaranteed access to an unlimited universe of new and fascinating experiences.

When in Rome, do as the Romans do

The proverb "When in Rome, do as the Romans do" defines a great strategy for gaining insight into another culture and opening the door to exciting and rewarding experiences.

Optimally, we should speak the local language. For travelers who visit many different countries, this is simply impossible. I have benefitted a lot from being multilingual, but there are thousands of languages and dialects in this world and one cannot learn them all. So often I have felt it was a shame that I couldn't dive deeper into a culture for lack of knowledge of the local language! However, just a couple of words learned quickly from a guidebook show people that you are open-minded and are trying to express at least the basic courtesies in the local language. People are grateful for this gesture, however clumsy it might be, because it is tangible proof that you came to get to know the culture.

It's not necessary to build arguments here for the importance of learning foreign languages or how functioning in more than one language sharpens the mind, widens one's horizons, and hones one's communication skills. The shelves of libraries and bookstores are full of books extolling the values of language studies. Even American President Barack Obama recently said, *"We should have every child speaking more than one language."*

But spoken language is not our sole means of communicating with others. It is well to remember the wise old sayings "behavior speaks for itself" and "actions are stronger than words". One can be completely fluent in a foreign language and communicate only negative messages, or worse, not communicate at all. One can learn how to communicate sensitivity and respect with a smile and a handshake as well words.

With a positive and open mind and using all our senses, it is easy to observe what the majority of people around you do and not do. That is the true meaning of "When in Rome..." Make yourself a part of what is going on around you and you will find complicity. It is not a secret that if you eat what local people eat, drink what they drink, sing what they sing, and dance what they dance, you will almost always be the perfect guest and the moments you share with the people around you will be among the most stimulating and rewarding of your life.

I have made discovering local cuisine and table customs a rule of thumb when travelling for business and have felt embarrassed when my hosts have invited me to eat out in the latest and most expensive foreign restaurant in town. They wanted to impress me with their international flair while I preferred to steep myself local culture! When possible, I try to subtly let my foreign colleagues know that an invitation to their favorite local restaurant would be a great honor.

When it comes to relationships between men and women and other culturally specific protocols, it is very wise to be extra alert and always err on the side of excessive respect for the other culture. Be open-minded and keep your eyes wide open every minute, but if the situation calls for it, you might have to look the other way to avoid problems. A catchy Romanian proverb gives good advice for travelling to places with very different codes of conduct: "If you are travelling in the blind man's country close one eye."

Going away is coming closer to yourself

Having a critical distance is useful in getting a closer view of the real things in life. When we travel and open ourselves up to foreign cultures, we learn more about ourselves. Our vision and understanding of our own personality and our native culture gets a fine tuning and we learn to see things from a different point of view.

The famous German poet Johann Wolfgang von Goethe was an inveterate and open-minded traveler who made a point of saying that one should not judge the world one does not know and who advocated having an objective opinion about one's own country before travelling abroad .The more we recognize the broad differences between cultures, and the more closely we observe the little details of each one, the more we might ask ourselves what we can learn from them. Believing that everything is better at home is often overestimating our home-grown values. We shouldn't base our judgments of other cultures on personal or cultural dogmas, national prejudices, or pre-conceived ideas. If we do, our ignorance will make us blind to the many interesting and enriching things we could learn. The writer Mark Twain summed this up when he said, "Travel is fatal to prejudice, bigotry & narrow mindedness. Broad, wholesome, charitable views cannot be acquired by vegetating in one little corner of the earth." Learning about others is learning about one's self and acquiring self awareness is an invaluable tool in making our way in the world.

Not every journey involves crossing time zones or changing latitudes

It is not the distance we travel from home that guarantees new discoveries and exciting moments. Great travel destinations are never far from us. Marcel Proust wrote: "The real voyage of discovery consists not in seeking new landscapes but in having new eyes." Crossing time zones and continents to have a change of scenery can be very worthwhile, but rediscovering landscapes nearer to us by giving them a closer look or seeing them through a new lens, can also be a useful and rewarding travel experience. The key is not "vegetating in one little corner of the world".

When I hear people say, "I'll explore the world closer to home when I get older or when I can't afford to travel abroad," I would love to advise them to give first priority to the things they can do without a lot of money while they still enjoy good physical health and a sound mind. Training our minds and developing good attitudes close to our own turf, we will prepare ourselves to get more out of long distance travel in the future. Don't put off until tomorrow the little pleasures you can have today. We never know what tomorrow will bring and we might not have a second chance.

Speed travelling blurs the big picture

Our life is marked by speed .We cook10 minute meals, gulp down our food, work against the clock, test the speed limit in our cars, indulge in quick sex and take package tours of ten cities in eight days. Instant food, instant love, instant performance, and instant money are just some examples of 21st century driven behavior. Speed is in and taking one's time is out. Although most of the quality experiences in life require time, we compulsively give priority to speed. This became our modus vivendi when we began to base our values on the misbegotten, one-dimensional belief that time is money and fell into the trap of thinking that speed always results in higher efficiency, greater dynamism, and more power.

Speed is the enemy of perception because speed blurs the big picture. When we travel, this blurring starts with the transport we choose to reach our destination. There is no doubt that if we only have a few weeks at our disposal to cross continents, high speed jets are the only way to go, but what our eyes can make out from a height of 10,000 meters above sea level will not give us a clear picture of where we're going or where we've been. We will have no real feeling for the changes in climate, weather, or vegetation, nor will we learn anything about the human beings living in the vast spaces we fly over. Almost the same thing happens when we travel by high speed rail. What we see through the window of a train cruising at 200 miles per hour leaves us with only the vaguest impressions of the cities and countryside we travel through.

When I peer out of the window of a plane, squinting my eyes to make out the most basic contours of the landscapes below me, I become jealous of Marco Polo and Ibn Battuta. They travelled thousands of miles on horseback, getting to know the roads and fields along the route and seeing, hearing, feeling, and smelling the exotic new things around them. Best of all, they arrived without jet lag!

Of course I am grateful for the travelling I have been able to do most of my life, but having logged in more miles than Marco Polo and Ibn Battuta is not the same as experiencing Mother Earth step by step and up close as they did. If you have the available time, I suggest that you consider travelling by foot, bicycle, motorbike, car, or a small sailing boat and get a feeling for the territory the way Marco Polo and Ibn Battuta did. Making stops at the interesting places you find along the way, you will tangibly enjoy every single mile of your journey. The experience will be much deeper and more intense for having direct experience with everything along the route. It's liberating to accept the fact that we can't be in all places at all times and to settle down to enjoying the journey itself. Travelling this way, the images that we take home in our minds will give us a bigger and clearer picture of where we've been.

Mind travel can help you balance your inner self with the world outside

It shouldn't surprise us that the mind can travel while the body stays at home. Mental travel helps us maintain a balance between our inner psychological and spiritual needs and the demands of our physical activities. We may travel in our dreams at night, but the more interesting and exciting travel I'm referring to is comprised of the journeys our conscious mind makes during our waking hours, journeys for which we consciously define the destination and in which we ourselves are the navigators setting out on an adventure, making a perfect landing, and generating our own excitement.

Neither am I making a reference to so-called "Astro Travelling". Many books and articles have been written about this concept, whose validity and benefits are open to discussion. I want to suggest another more practical and rewarding method of strengthening your mind's capacity to raise you above the limitations of what may seem to be unpleasant or boring moments and help you to create personal mental retreats where you can go to find pleasure and peace when you need it. If you know how to spread the wings of your mind and direct your thoughts toward more pleasurable and edifying ideas, you can transform many negative situations into positive experiences. It's a matter of keeping a balance between your inner and outer lives and developing automatic self-defense mechanisms against oncoming negative feelings or depression.

I'm not talking about day dreaming either. Daydreaming is passive reverie. The mind can soar much higher than a daydream's flights of fancy. If you put the triple mind alliance to work for you, you will no longer seek to escape reality because you will often be able to mitigate or transform the seemingly negative reality around you through a balanced partnership of your innermost self and the world around you.

Our mind is an incredible private universe to travel in. In terms of individual freedom, it is the only really free and democratic place you will experience in your life. Your mind is the bastion of your personal definitions of duty and privilege. It can tell you instinctively where to go to find peace, inspiration, ideas, or excitement. Let it lead you to interesting destinations, whether you are in an armchair traveler mode or cooling your heels in a line at the post office. That is not to say that you should be on another planet when your boss, spouse, son, or daughter is trying to tell you something important. It's great to have a private mental beach to go to when you need a time out from the daily routine, but we all must learn to catch the wave at the right moment to avoid emotional wipe-outs. If you can learn to balance your mental travel with the rhythm and demands of world around you, you will achieve a higher level of harmony in your life.

The unlimited universe of our minds is a source from which we can draw upon not only our personal experience, but also our genetic inheritance and the legacy of collective experience. All are registered in our personal HARD & HEART DISKs. Your brain's supercomputer takes into account all of your preferences, from your genetic predispositions to your most personally held beliefs, and has stored the memory of everything you have learned and lived since your brain started to develop in your mother's womb. This personal mental archive offers an unbelievable quantity of information that you can refer to and benefit from, and functions as a clearinghouse for what I call **our personal affinity-mindset zones or AMZs.**

Your affinity-mindset zones are conceptual mental spaces organized categorically by your preferences, experiences, and beliefs where you can go to relax, dream, be inspired, or make necessary periodic adjustments to your moods and your general state of mind. They are full of useful information and entertaining ideas for personal inner journeys. Time spent in your mind's AMZs will involve diving deep into your subconscious and awakening a lot of feelings that may have been stored deep in the recesses of your mind for years. The subconscious level of the mind is what psychologists explore to bring our hidden memories and feelings to the surface in order to help us overcome traumas and phobias. If we learn to maintain contact with our subconscious minds and nourish them, we are doing our health a favor. Let's have a closer look at how the concept of affinity-mindset zones functions and how it can help you identify the key elements for embarking on rewarding inner journeys.

What are affinity-mindset zones and why should we visit them?

Each person has a variety of AMZs that are organized according to the variables of his education, upbringing, and personal physical and mental experiences. We may share some affinities and mindsets with others, but each of us will have developed unique combinations of mentalities and affinities that make up our specific personalities. What may bore or excite us may differ greatly from what bores or excites other people from almost identical personal backgrounds. The concept of AMZs can be used to identify what really interests us, stimulate our mental activity, and help us to maintain a variety of mental retreats where we can go to immerse ourselves in our own core interests. If we have developed a positive, open, and active mind we will have already instinctively identified a variety of personal AMZs that can serve as gateways to mood- boosting, tailor-made inner experiences.

How your mindset affects your inner and outer life

Tell me what motivates you in life and I will tell you what you most often do and where you most often go. I would only be using logical deduction, but that's what a healthy mind does. If you establish a positive mindset and use it as a filter for your thoughts and actions, you are more likely to be in a good mood. This is a good reason for visiting your affinity-mindset zones as often as possible. Taking a tour of the different affinity-mindset zones described below, you will find yourself more at home in some than in others, because they represent your strong affinity for certain activities, environments, philosophies, and movements you can personally identify with. You might want to make your own private affinity-mindset profile as you go along to use as a guide in the future.

Now let's visit some classic affinity-mindset zones, or AMZs.

The Travel AMZ

Our mind condenses and stores memories of all our life travels in its own custom-made travel catalogue, from our first steps to our trips around the world. To the existing catalogue of firsthand memories, we can add files based on the second-hand information we have absorbed from books, magazines, movies, and television. We can even create wish lists of our travel fantasies to dream about in a moment of sadness or boredom. All this mental organization makes mind travel easier and more fun. Once we are seasoned travelers in our minds, we might even get the body interested in coming along next time. Mental voyages can help us to plan our ultimate dream trip better and then make it come true. As Oscar Hammerstein wrote in lyrics for the Broadway musical South Pacific, "If you don't have a dream, how are you going to make a dream come true?" Even if mind travelling is the only form of travelling available to you due to your health or your financial situation, remember that many of our best travel dreams can be lived out in our hearts and minds without ever leaving home.

The Culture AMZ

What would our life be without art, music, theatre, or dance? We have music in our head almost from our conception. Within our mother's womb we live to the beat of her heart, and well before birth we are sensitive and responsive to her voice and other ambient sounds. The lullabies our mothers sang us to sleep with were the first concerts we attended. Growing up, music accompanies the most important moments of our life. Hearing a song that brings back strong memories can even move us to tears. We often start singing or humming our favorite melodies when we listen to the radio and music sets our feet tapping, urging us to dance. Music is a principle determinant to our moods and a universal language we can share with others worldwide. The German poet, writer, and philosopher Friedrich Nietzsche defined the importance he personally gave to music in the aphorism: "Without music, life would be a mistake."

For composers and musicians, a visit to a personal AMZ Concert Hall might inspire a new composition or interpretation, but it can be a great source of joy for everyone. Just closing our eyes and letting music take us far away is a journey worth repeating again and again.

There is a potential artist or a craftsman in each of us. No one is born without some innate ability for creating or inventing and a desire to express what he has felt and seen. Children instinctively desire to draw on every surface within their reach.

Visual artists have highly developed AMZs. They spend years accumulating visions, inspirations, and technical skills. Transforming all this material into a work of art requires a refining process that can only be carried out in the recesses of the inner mind. Artists are masters in developing their own tailor-made AMZs. They spend their lives balancing their inner visions with everyday reality. They are constant practitioners of the daily in-depth reflection and find inspiration in the most common objects. Look what Andy Warhol did with only a Campbell's soup can!

Some artists travel all over the world to find their inspiration, while others create their own worlds at home. From the 1930s until his death in 1973, artist Joseph Cornell created delicate, mysterious, and beautiful collages and sculptural boxes that gave new life to small objects found in second-hand stores and the streets of New York. Cornell was forced to abandon his formal education to help out in the family dry-goods business, and after his father died, he supported his mother and cared for his severely handicapped brother. He created his artwork on the margin of his heavy family responsibilities but was never an amateur or a dabbler. A collector of what he called "ephemera" – old magazines and prints, stamps, and other odd assorted bits of things–he researched every little object he brought home. Although he had only a secondary school education, he became an expert on a wide range of worldly topics, spurred by his curiosity in the story behind the printed materials and objects he worked with. The magical and unique works of art he created are now in major collections all over the world. Looking at them, one would imagine that Cornell had spent a lifetime travelling to exotic places, but he spent almost his entire lifetime in New York City, making only occasional visits to Nyack or Long Island. His personal AMZ must have been not only a place to sort out endless creative decisions, but a refuge from his demanding family responsibilities as well.

There are many other arts that we can practice or enjoy as an appreciative public, such as dance and theatre. The arts are a great way to nourish a positive, open, and active mind and we should all visit our culture AMZ frequently.

The Wellness AMZ

Wellness and wellbeing activities and treatments are in these days. In fact, they never went out of style, particularly the mental treatment and training we need to give ourselves to maintain a healthy and positive mindset. Sophisticated marketing techniques and technological innovations have brought wellness to the mass marketplace and made it a profitable, mainstream industry but the concept and its essentials have been with us for thousands of years. The essentials are the same now as they were in ancient times: a quiet lake, birdsong, the sound of wind rustling the leaves of a tree, or a bubbling brook or fountain. All have the divine effect of relaxing the body and the mind.

In our wellness AMZ we can mentally walk along peaceful, deserted beaches or playback a memory of the sound of wind in the pines. Such a refreshing visit will hopefully inspire us to make time for the real thing: direct communion with the real nature outside.

The Religious AMZ

It is not difficult to convince true believers to make daily visits to their own, personal, spiritual AMZ. Even if one is not a member of any particular religion, he or she might feel the urge for regular spiritual contemplation.

In a very materialistic world, it is healthy to set aside time to devote our minds to higher, more spiritual thinking.

People feel emotionally connected to the outward trappings of their religious identities and feel more spiritually linked to a supreme divine power when participating in group ceremonies surrounded by familiar religious icons. We can also, however, visit the church, mosque, temple, or synagogue inside us. It is a place to visit in moments of faith, doubt, jubilation, and deep sadness alike. If we enter with an open heart, it can even be a more sincere pilgrimage than a physical visit to a physical place. Praying for specific things to happen, and giving thanks for wonderful moments we have lived, are acts common to most religions and are, in fact, the core of a religious mentality. A person with a religious mindset prays wherever and whenever he finds himself. I recently met an elderly woman in a little Spanish village. She expressed her concerns about her husband's health and wondered how she would be able to handle all of life's daily problems alone. Being both a convinced believer and a practical woman, she explained her own religious mindset to me through a proverb: *À Dios rogando y con el mazo dando* (Ask God for help but work hard to make things happen). This proverb shows the wisdom of maintaining a healthy equilibrium between of our inner mental state and the physical reality we must face every day.

The Sports AMZ

Many people have a sports AMZ they visit many times a day throughout their lives. Sporting events and sports heroes live on in the minds of fans long after the lights have gone out in the stadium and the heroes have retired from the game. Fans like to remember the most exciting moments of their favorite teams and players, and people who have played sports themselves take pleasure in recalling their prowess and the camaraderie shared with their teammates.

The emotional fever of the fans that fill stadiums is shared by many others in front of television screens. Sporting events are no doubt a mental escape from the boring daily routine for many people. Even if the morning and afternoon seem to us to have been a total loss, if our team wins in the evening, it transforms the day into a day of victory.

For many young people, their sports AMZ is a place to go to dream of the future. Without a strong inner vision nurtured daily, no young athlete could make an Olympic dream come true.

The Hollywood and Prime Time AMZ

Since the early nineteen-twenties, Hollywood has been a dream factory that has influenced cultures across the world. It has taken us to faraway places and sparked our imaginations. Nowadays, television networks fighting for audience share produce dramatic series that invite people to escape from their own not always rosy daily lives and other studio centers like Bollywood, in India, bring us fresh and lively versions of the ever-repeating stories of boy meets girl and cops and robbers.

Our Hollywood and prime time affinity-mindset zone can be our own personal studio where we are the producers, directors, and stars. Who hasn't pictured him or herself as Rhett Butler or Scarlett O'Hara, or dreamed of replicating the Kung Fu exploits of Jackie Chan? These days, almost anyone can edit their home videos and photos and post them on social internet sites. Many people love to make clever Power Point presentations that they send to their friends via internet. Non-professionals even provide news channels with their own news-breaking footage of things they have personally witnessed. The Hollywood and prime time AMZ is a place to go to think up bright new ideas for productions that could end up being more exciting than what we see in movie theatres and on television!

The Love AMZ

Falling in love is wonderful, but experts say that romantic love only lasts on the average a few years and psychologists now tell us that companionate love, that many used to think began to grow as romantic love slowly waned, also declines precipitously over time. This would be depressing news if it were not for the theory of psychologist Robert J. Sternberg, Dean of the School of Arts and Sciences of Tufts University and author of a very interesting book titled *Love is a story*.

Dr. Sternberg believes that love between two people can be sustained many years, "but in order for it to flourish, both partners must share the same love story". Sternberg was fascinated by the fact that most people identified strongly with love stories and actively followed the love stories they found in books, magazines, television, and the movies. He discovered that the more people's stories matched, the longer their relations continued to be fulfilling. This theory squares perfectly with what we have discussed in this book about the importance of making the evening an important part of our day and confirms what maintaining an active romance AMZ can do for your personal relations.

We might want to return to the prior discussion of Hollywood-prime time AMZs. Remember the final scene of "Gone with the Wind"? It's a classic example of how relations between two people who shared many affinities fell apart. At a critical juncture in their relations, Rhett and Scarlet fail to buy into a common love story. In the very moment that Scarlet realizes that she is really in love with Rhett, she quotes her adolescent love, Ashley. The rest is movie history.

Creating a common story means using the resources of all our AMZs and paying an occasional visit to the AMZs of those we love. Special anniversary dinners and champagne and roses are wonderful, but the secret to creating a lasting shared love story is respecting the mindset and supporting the affinities of the other person. It requires very little effort for a woman to look up from her magazine to celebrate a televised goal with her husband. It shouldn't be so difficult for a man to show interest in a new dress his wife has just brought home. These fleeting moments and how we live them determine whether we suffer years of a slow death of the soul or accumulate many exciting moments that double our satisfaction with our lives. Occasional flowers and champagne are the icing on the cake, not the bread and butter we need every day to live.

The same imperative of maintaining synchronized life and love stories applies to our relations with other people we love: our parents, our children, and our close friends. Yes, Grandmother has repeated the same story a million times. No, we don't really want to attend the parents' day meeting or all of the sports events our children participate in. When our love relations are strained, we should spend a few minutes in our love AMZ and remember the father who taught us to ride a bicycle, our first date with our husband or wife, or the first steps of our son or daughter. Taking up the thread of our shared love story from a happy moment, instead of dwelling on a moment of temporary discord, can help us achieve the positive and enduring life narratives we all seek.

Using the natural synchronicity between our AMZs to enrich our relationships and our lives

Some of our personal AMZs will naturally be less important than others in helping us achieve an inner and outer life balance and get more joy out of life, but once we are aware of our personal affinities and are conscious of our individual mindsets, we will be better equipped to channel our thinking positively and manage our moods better. Mental cross-fertilization of our AMZs is a great technique for creating a more positive mindset that will lead us to more exciting ideas and more extraordinary moments. Instead of thinking, "I hate this routine; I am tired of this relationship; I just can't do any better," use the positive energy you have gained in your daily reflection and in your AMZs to affirm, "I love what I do; I'm going to put new life into this relationship; and Yes, I can!" Happiness is a state of mind. If we make a little time to cultivate our affinities and recognize the affinities of those around us every day, we will be happier travelers on life's journey.

21ˢᵗ century virtual travel: Mindsets & Mind Sites

There is another great place to go to cultivate our affinities, entertain ourselves, and get informed: THE WORLD WIDE WEB. It deserves to be written in capital letters because it represents capital progress in global communication. There is practically no information on earth that can't be found by navigating the Internet. Internet functions a lot like our affinity-mindset zones. Our mind selects a theme, and with the introduction of a few key words or phrases, thousands of new navigation routes light up the screen.

Internet is a combination of the greatest public library in history, an audio-visual megastore, an international game room and a 24 hour chat room. It is a unique multimedia learning system and anyone with internet access, a strong will, and the necessary discipline to stick with it could theoretically earn a university degree in almost any field of study in its virtual classrooms.

Navigating the web can also easily become an endless escape from real life, because the structure of the virtual world is very similar to that of a daydream. Questioning the tremendous value of this medium, however, would be a sign of ignorance and definitive proof of not being connected to the world we live in today.

The Internet is a great medium for learning to spread our wings and take flight, but I am completely convinced that it cannot substitute real life experiences. Remember that our triple mind alliance–the positive mind, open mind, and active mind–is our means of avoiding the garbage in, garbage out syndrome when we cruise the web.

What we get out of the Internet is our choice and our responsibility. To what extent our digital escapes provide us with information, inspiration, and "feel good" moments strongly depends on what our positive, open, and active mind tells us to download. The Internet can enrich our lives if we use our mind to upgrade the service it provides. Our positive, open, and active minds will also help us to upload our thoughts and share our knowledge through personal sites, blogs, chats, personal web pages, and networking sites. Interacting through social networking sites or opinion blogs is the greatest opportunity we have ever had to find other people who share our interests and to interchange opinions with other human beings all over the world. Even if you never take a plane to India, via Internet, you could get to know a taxi driver from Madras!

If you're planning a trip, researching your destination in Internet is a great travel-planning tool. You can find webcam views of famous places, read other traveler's opinions of hotels and restaurants you are considering, find out whether you need a visa, and check the exchange rate. When you return home, you can add your comments to travel sites to help fellow travelers and upload your travel photos to share your experience with others. While on the road, however, go "unplugged" and dedicate your mind and all your senses to savoring the adventure.

The Internet is almost as magic and unlimited as our minds, but it has a limitation that it will never overcome: Our mind thinks, the Internet only informs. Our minds are connected to all our senses in a way that Internet will never be able to replicate, however sophisticated it becomes. Last, but not least, the mind is a private and secure place. No one can hack their way into our thoughts. Nothing we experience in the digital world will be as perfect, as pleasurable, or as private as what we experience in our own minds.

Last call for the gates

Now that we've visited the affinity-mindset zones of our minds and learned to make good use of them, we are ready for the next step. We will now move from the mindset to the daily role of our MIND IN THE SETTING to see how we can use our new mental prowess to beat the monotony and turn "life as usual" into extraordinary moments and more joy of living.

With our positive, open, and active minds ready to take off on a new life adventure, we are ready to go to the gates. It could be the last minute call to catch the most important flight we will ever take.

PART II: "THE MIND IN THE SETTING"

From "As Usual" boredom to "exceptional experiences"

"How is everything today?" "As usual, thank you!" This is a routine question that elicits a routine answer. The problem is that our "as usual" lives don't offer us anything new to talk about. If our days are always monotonous, boring, uninspiring, or even worse, de-motivating or depressing, what kind of excitement can we expect to have in our lives?

If there is no excitement in our lives, life loses it flavor. An "as usual" attitude towards life shuts the mind's door to inspiration and creativity and leaves us on a pre-programmed path to boredom. When we can't give any other answer to "How is everything", it's time to act. This is a crucial moment to add some excitement to our personal relations before they go stale, or even sour.

Relationships need salt and pepper

If young couples contemplating marriage in many Western countries today read the latest statistics on divorce before they tied the knot, they might think twice before buying their wedding bands and hiring a caterer. More than 50 percent of marriages celebrated today with vows to stay together until "death do us part" won't last 15 years. Despite the gloomy statistics, the hope of attaining everlasting love can be realized if one has the will to make a marriage succeed and the right techniques for sustaining the original magic. Less than one hundred percent commitments don't deserve to be called love and should be given a different name.

I recently heard an interesting definition of what makes an authentic entrepreneur. A real entrepreneur starts his projects with the same conviction that a person truly in love brings to a marriage. If one doesn't have the will to make the union prosperous, the chances of a happy ending are small. Believing in something is all about making dreams happen, not just sitting around moping and hoping.

Many books have been written about how to keep love alive, how to avoid a bitter breakup, or how to re-conquer a lost love. More than ever, professional relationship specialists (and those who pretend to be) work hard to maintain the myth that love just happens. If these so-called love specialists made a career change the world would be better off.

This book does not intend to be yet another guide to a happy marriage but to simply point out that one of the greatest factors in the loss of attraction between two people is the boredom of their daily routines. Research and life experience confirm that the value of efforts made to keep mutual attraction alive cannot be overestimated.

When one feels the boredom of "as usual" creeping into his or her relationship, a lack of appeal and a lessening of personal involvement might not be far off. Sharing exciting moments instead of living out a boring eternity together is vital in keeping personal relationships pulsing. Mr. and Mrs. High Aspirations should never become Mr. and Mrs. As Usual.

When Mr. and Mrs. High Aspirations turn into Mr. and Mrs. "As Usual"

It is common knowledge that in spite of good intentions, in most cases the blush is off the rose of human passion in only a few years. Daily life, with its habits, work stress, and the drag of personal responsibilities, can easily become an invariable routine, devoid of beauty and inspiration. Routine is an invisible virus that slowly and silently insinuates itself into our lives and nurtures itself on our complacent or defeatist attitudes and thoughts. If unattended to, the virus gets under our skin and circulates to our hearts and minds, convincing us that we are helpless against its power and leaving emotional scars. Lethargy in human relationships needs immediate treatment before it transforms itself into a deeply-rooted sense of dissatisfaction.

If we are aware from the very beginning what is happening to us, we can consciously protect ourselves from the deadening of our emotions by taking the right measures to keep love alive. However, if the routine reaches the contagious stage and both people are affected, what can be done? Give in to temptation of thinking that the ring feels too tight on one's finger? Not at all! Nothing is as lost as it appears to be in a moment of desperation. Let's talk about how to bring excitement back to our relationships, starting with the dinner table. It might be that a little salt and pepper is all that is needed to set things right again.

Around, at, on, and under the table

 Bon Appétit, Buen Provecho, Enjoy your meal, Guten Appetit , and Bel Hana wel Shefaa are just a few of the thousands of similar wishes that are spoken aloud at tables around the world. They are wonderful expressions of the joy of sitting down together, not just to eat, but also to be close and share the company of friends and family. Sharing one of life's greatest pleasures is a ceremony that requires the sufficient time to savor everything.

Let's take a couple of moments to reflect about the act and art of eating and the time and attention that should be given to it. One of the worst errors we make when we eat is not dedicating the attention and time the meal deserves. Doctors, nutritionists, cooks, and lifestyle specialists are always telling us that we should eat slowly in a relaxing atmosphere and be consciousness of enjoying every bite, because eating is an act of love for ourselves. Eating is a highly sensorial celebration for both our bodies and our minds. Devouring a good meal in record time is, first of all, an offence to the person who dedicated time, skill, and personal effort in preparing it. Secondly, it deprives us of an essential pleasure. Eating too quickly is also a form of self-punishment, as it is likely to leave us emotionally unsatisfied and can provoke indigestion. Voltaire described the yin and yang of food when he said: "Nothing would be more tiresome than eating and drinking if God had not made them a pleasure as well as a necessity".

It doesn't make sense to pack a lot of less important gatherings into our day only to end up not having time to sit down and enjoy what should be our number one pleasure. We could learn a lot from societies that have highly developed gastronomic cultures and consider eating a form of art. In these cultures, people have a social and culinary-oriented attitude toward time management and demand time to enjoy and share the principal meals of the day as a natural part of their schedules. It's no coincidence that these societies enjoy high levels of family and social cohesion and high coefficients of life satisfaction.

The Slow Food movement embraces the concept of eating healthy local products and preserving both traditional methods of preparing and cooking food and the traditional custom of making every meal a celebration. Founded in the 1980s by Italian Carlo Petrini as a protest against fast food, it has become an international organization dedicated to preserving and promoting unique regional products and reviving the almost forgotten tradition of fully savoring a well prepared meal. Who amongst us would refute the assertion that a simmering casserole made with fresh, regional products is tastier, healthier, and more satisfying than fast food?

What's on the table (and who is around it) at meal time can be a barometer of our quality of life. Taking time out to eat well is a way of reawakening and training our senses and sharing quality time with friends and loved ones. I personally believe that sitting down at the table together is a crucial element in establishing and maintaining relationships, particularly private and family relationships. Not investing the time or having an interest in sharing a meal with people is not investing the time or having an interest in maintaining a relevant level of personal involvement with them. Topics that are not discussed and solved around the table will be difficult to solve elsewhere.

The table is an intimate social space in many cultures around the world. It is the stage for high drama, confrontation, and celebration and is one of the best places to make a deal. Clasping hands across a table or engaging in a little game of footsy under the table has solidified many new flirtations and awakened the dying embers of many fading passions. Let's give the table the place of honor and the time it deserves and make it the largest and richest buffet of exciting moments on Earth. There is no better spot to toast proposals for new adventures and relive happy memories with those you love.

Fusion Fantasy Food Unlimited!

Early in childhood we get used to familiar dishes and that's fine if what we eat is healthy and we are born into a culture that is blessed with a great culinary tradition. But with all respect to even the most gastronomically-oriented cultures on earth, if you always eat the same things, mealtime can become a boring routine. Eating the same rice, potatoes, and pasta with same old herbs and sauces day after day is falling into a culinary rut. Little changes in our favorite recipes can give our dishes, and our spirits, a big lift.

Food fusion, the combining of ingredients and techniques of various cultures to create exciting, new dishes, is one of the most interesting culinary innovations of the last few decades. It's relatively easy to do and only requires a few non-standard products that can be found in larger supermarkets and specialty stores. Creative cooking is no longer the privilege of a select group of five star chefs. You can become a star in your own kitchen and have fun setting a festive mood with table decorations, candles, and the right music. There are many television shows and magazines dedicated to cookery that can give you ideas and teach you the basic techniques you lack to make truly memorable meals.

Travelling and eating out you will discover that, wherever you go in the world, the basic food products are very similar. The culinary differences from one country to another lie in the spices, the methods of preparation, and the way the food is presented. Many of the greatest new stars in the gastronomic world have not come out the top culinary schools. They have simply developed their natural affinity for all things culinary through curiosity, diligence, and hard work. You might want to create a personal affinity-mindset zone for storing up tips from the experts and dreaming up new innovations of your own. The kitchen is a great place to cross new frontiers and even test our limits.

Let's reconsider the possibilities of those traditional staples pasta, potatoes, and rice and start creating our own exciting fusions based on them. Pasta, potatoes, and rice are the stars of the contemporary food fusion movement and we could easily eat one of them each and every day without being bored or breaking our budgets. Starting from a base of these three staples, we'll apply the **7 x 7 x 8 formula** that can be used to create a new, exciting fusion dish every day of the year, leap-year included.

Three ways to beat boredom in the kitchen: pasta mania, potato mania, and rice mania

Pasta: the Queen of fusion

Some historic facts about the queen:

Although our friend Marco Polo is widely reputed to have introduced pasta to Europe from China, it is more likely that it was introduced to the continent by the Arab conquerors of Sicily. The first known written record of cooking it in boiling water appears in the Jerusalem Talmud, in the 5th century A.D. The great Italian film director Federico Fellini said, "Life is a combination of magic and pasta". For the health and figure-conscious, Sophia Loren is perhaps the greatest living advertisement for eating pasta in the world. In her delightful cookbook *Recipes and Memories,* she recounts how Hollywood reporters wanting to know the secret of her marvelous figure were surprised when she told them that she ate pasta almost every day.

Pasta can be combined with almost anything and the following exercise will prove to you in minutes how you can create your own delicious pasta fusion without losing any of any of the nutritional benefits Sophia Loren swears by. It's easy to create a pasta dish for almost every personal taste. Don't forget that there are more types of pasta than we can count. There are spinach and tomato pastas that add color and flavor to the dish, whole wheat pastas for those who are looking for healthier, more natural meal options, and regional varieties like couscous that are incredibly easy to prepare. Now there are even gluten-free pastas for people who suffer gluten intolerance.

Once you've chosen your pasta, select one of the following seven basic protein choices to complement it: diced veal, chicken, fish, pork, lamb, turkey, or shrimp. The next choice will determine the overall flavor, so think carefully before selecting one of the following seven classic world sauces: tomato, curry, soy, mayonnaise, peanut butter, melted cheese, and béchamel. You've already begun to learn the art of mixing, but the creativity of fusion mania continues...

The next choice will be between eight vegetables (always better when fresh): The first time out, you may want to select just one of the eight great vegetables on this list: tomato, beans, peas, carrots, onions, sprouts, broccoli, or chili pepper; but soon you'll be coming up with ideas for adding more. Remember that you are not only adding flavor and color, but lots of healthy vitamins as well!

Gourmet mathematicians have calculated that varying the combinations of the 3 basic ingredient groups noted above one can create up to 392 different food fusion entrees! Don't be shy and try your hand at creating a totally unique number 393.

The Website: **www.proexciting moments.com** is the place to find a fusion pasta recipe or share your own personal recipes with other "pasta maniacs".

Potato: the king of fusion

Some historic facts about the king:

The potato, whose Latin name is *solanum tuberosum*, was first cultivated in the highlands of Peru more than 7,000 years ago. Its indigenous name, "papa", is still used interchangeably with the Spanish word *patata* throughout South America. Potatoes were brought to Europe from South America in the 16th century by the Spanish and over time became an important staple in the diets of many countries. A wonderful addition to the world's diet, a medium-sized unskinned potato is packed with an impressive 27 mg of vitamin C – 45% of the daily recommended dose of that vitamin. The potato took time to enter French and Spanish cookbooks, but now millions of kilos of "pommes frites", better known outside France as French fries, are sold every day and the Spanish tortilla, really a potato omelet, is one of the motors behind the current rage for tapas.

The same principal for creating pasta fusions can be applied to whip up creative new potato dishes. There are many varieties of potatoes and many ways to prepare them. Try steaming or frying them for a change from mashed potatoes. Apply the previously outlined 7 x 7 x 8 formula and make your own contribution to the great potato saga. Don't forget to look for ideas or post your potato fusion recipes in the website: **www. proexciting moments.com**

Rice: the Emperor of fusion

Some historic facts about the emperor:

Rice is a true star of culinary fusion. It has been cultivated for almost 10,000 years in Asia and was a staple crop in Africa and the Middle East long before its arrival in Europe. It arrived in South Carolina in 1694 and is still cultivated in the Mississippi River Delta. Rice feeds far more people in the world than potatoes and pasta. The pride of place it is given in all the great cuisines of the world attest to its truly imperial status.

You can apply the same principle of adding one of the seven protein basics, one of the seven great world sauces, and one or more of the eight mentioned vegetables to create up to 392 exciting rice recipes, more than one for every day of the year. Those who have never been able to cook a perfect pot of rice shouldn't give up. There are electric rice cookers on the market that will give you a perfect pot of rice every time and can be used to cook many other things as well, including porridge! Once again, share your recipe with others or find rice mania inspiration in the website: **www. proexciting moments.com**

It should be obvious that I am not suggesting restricting your diet to only pasta, potatoes, and rice year round, but the formula shows that regardless of the family budget or a cook's lack of experience, with a little creativity, meals don't have to be boring and repetitive. Fusion cuisine is about reaching out to other cultures to enrich your own. If you're reading this book in China, why not try to cook rice the way they cook it in Spain, just for a change? If you're reading this book in Spain, why not look up an Indian recipe in Internet, download some Ravi Shankar sitar music, and dedicate one Saturday afternoon to creating a Bollywood fantasy meal?

An open, active mind and a bit of work are all that are needed to create unlimited gourmet moments to share with others. We will now turn our attention to the table where the celebration takes place, and where little touches of sophistication can provide exciting evenings at home.

Culinary mind-travel and celebrations at home

One of the most memorable experiences of travelling is discovering and sharing the local cuisine in an incredible location. Preparing a weekend dinner party that celebrates a different culture can be a fun escape without leaving home. An African dinner at sunset on the Savannah of Kenya, for example, would be a really exciting experience for someone in another part of the world. For someone in Nairobi, a taste of Patagonia would be an exotic escape. Through a change of cuisine, we can experience at least some of the feeling of travelling to another country without physically going there while at the same time adding spice to our "as usual" day.

You can bring Africa into your dining room anywhere in the world, and even if it is obviously not the same as being on safari, at least you won't need a passport or spend a lot of money. Imagine saying Karibu kwa Chakula! (Welcome and enjoy the food! in the Kikuyu language), as your friends walk in the door. Why not try your hand at preparing a first course of Groundnut (peanut) soup and a second course of Githeri, a puree made of peas, corn, and potatoes seasoned with onions, garlic, coriander leaves, tomatoes, salt, and ghee (clarified butter), a gastronomic delight of the Kikuyu, Kenya's largest ethnic group. The Githeri could be served with Nyama choma - roast lamb. Exploring the many coffees of the world is a great way of travelling without leaving home. Kilimanjaro coffee would be a nice final touch to your African meal. It might sound like too much of a hassle to get all of this organized but, in fact, it is not much work for a special evening that everyone will remember.

This is just an example of the unlimited menus and settings that you can create at home. You could opt for Patagonia instead of the African savannah. If the cold of Patagonia makes you shiver at the idea, light a fire in the fireplace, if you have one, or listen to a CD of tango music. Cook up some King Prawns and open up a bottle of Argentinean Cabernet-Malbec and you have an escape to paradise.

If you are feeling really adventurous, you can travel the spice route: the exotic corners, islands or coasts of the Indian Ocean. Are you ready to add the spice of curry, cardamom, tamarind, and cloves to your life?

Imagine you are in Kerala, in the paradisiacal south of India, a region blessed with golden sunshine and embraced by the Indian Ocean. Kerala has an almost incomparable abundance of flora and fauna that has attracted explorers and merchants from over the world for centuries. The region has been a major exporter of fine spices–a hallmark of the rich local cuisine–for more than a thousand years. Kerala's natural beauty, fine food, and sensual spiritualism are only three of many reasons to make a delicious Kerala dinner the centre of your mind-travel journey to India. Indian spices and food products can be found in specialty markets to help you prepare a delicious Indian meal at home, but the most important ingredients are the right mood, a heartfelt desire to fly far away, and a little passion for something new and exciting.

A perfect way to get into the right mood and whet your appetite could be listening to the very sensitive and emotional traditional music of Kerala that easily can be found through the Internet. The traditional music of Kerala evolved from the music performed in its temples in ancient times. The Panchavadyam, with its five percussion instruments, provides a perfect musical backdrop for a traditional Keralan meal.

You might want to look for Indian tableware, such as place mats, wooden bowls and spoons made from coconuts, in a local import store to add to the atmosphere. Below is a simple reference guide to the many facets of Kerala cuisine. There are thousands of cookbooks and culinary websites where you can find detailed recipes, but your most important guides will be your curiosity and your five senses.

Kerala cuisine is based on a combination of vegetables, meat, and seafood flavored with various spices. The primary spices used by Kerala chefs are chilies, pepper, fenugreek, tamarind, and cardamom. A typical full course meal, served on a banana leaf, will have more than 14 dishes. The main menu may include boiled and cooked rice with Avial (a combination of vegetables, chicken drumstick, green chili peppers and coconut paste); Thoren (a dry curry dish made from chopped vegetables, coconut, fried green chilies, mustard seed, turmeric and curry leaves); Sambar (a spicy dish that includes lentils, onions, turmeric, coriander, and chicken drumsticks) and Olen (a mix of spiced beans and gourds). This may be followed by Rasam (a delicious clear broth believed to be good for the digestion). Dessert might be Payasam (sugared rice) or Pachadi (a combination of pumpkin and coconut milk with a touch of green chilly).

These are just a few examples of how we can travel around the world without leaving our own kitchens. The creativity we put into these meals, and improvisations we make, are more important than complete culinary authenticity. That's what Fusion cuisine is all about!

If your company has told you that you must learn a foreign language, make studying that language more interesting by experimenting with the cuisine related to it. This is an example of how jotting things down and posting them can really pay off. Fill your kitchen with vocabulary sticky notes for everything you will need, and need to do, to create a meal in the language you are studying. Listen to a recording of music in that language while you are preparing the meal. This will help you to forge a positive "yes, I can" mindset toward learning the most difficult language and set a great mood for the meal. It's a perfect way to balance the seemingly contrary demands of your inner and outer lives.

The concept of an exotic dinner at home is not just for adults and their invited guests. Planning a series of international meals that coincide with your children's geography and history studies is a great way to deepen their interest in foreign cultures and spend quality time with them, from researching the recipes to decorating the table and choosing the music. Exploring new worlds together is also a good way for everyone in the family to widen his or her horizons and an excellent tactic for preventing children from losing their sense of spontaneity and sense of wonder.

We prepare special foods and perform special rituals for our own ethnic and national holidays. Why not extend our list of holiday traditions to include celebrations that are entirely new to us? The Japanese have fallen in love with Christmas just for the fun of it. Why not adopt a Japanese holiday for just one year to have a change of pace? Trying one's hand at origami, the Japanese art of paper folding, could result in some very original decorations, and a wok might be a fun and healthy addition to your kitchen pots and pans.

If you're not ready to adopt an entire holiday, even adding one international detail like a Mexican piñata to a child's birthday party can make the event more special. A piñata is nothing more than paper maché applied to an inflated balloon. If you make your own, you can fill it with treats you have chosen yourself.

New Year is fun to celebrate and a perfect moment to make new resolutions. Since different cultures celebrate the New Year at different times of the year, we can combine new resolutions with new culinary escapes the whole year round. If we haven't had enough New Year when it is celebrated according to the Julian calendar, we can start again with the same festivities when the Gregorian calendar celebrates the beginning of the year a few weeks later. Chinese New Year normally falls in the month of February. The Persian New Year is timed to coincide with the exact moment of the vernal equinox, which usually occurs in late March, and is often celebrated with picnics in the country. The various cultures that make up India all have different dates for their New Year's celebrations, and as the Muslim calendar is based on a lunar year of 354 days, once in a blue moon there are two Muslim New Years in one Western calendar year! Rosh Hashanah, the Jewish New Year, is celebrated in September by eating symbolic foods, such as apples and honey. It's good to remember that every day, in some corner of the world, people are gathering together to celebrate life, make new resolutions, and break the routine.

Even when we aren't celebrating an official holiday or indulging in a fusion food fantasy, we should make the most of our opportunities to sit down at the table together. Weekend mornings are full of precious culinary moments that we let slip away from us. Is heading out to the shopping mall right away really your top priority? A leisurely family breakfast might be more rewarding. Try dripping pancake batter to form shapes on the griddle; one glop to make a head and two more strategically placed to make ears and you have a recognizable Mickey Mouse that will make the most finicky child sit down and eat. Freshly squeezed orange juice, freshly ground coffee, and butter curls decorating a plate of toast can revive last night's romantic mood and set a magic tone for the entire day. Remember to make time for your morning candy.

Whether you plan a romantic dinner for two, a dinner party for friends, or an intimate family get together, these special, out of the ordinary meals will have a very positive side effect: from the preparation that will spark your creativity and heighten our awareness of your own or other cultures, to the memorable moments shared with friends and family, you will be adding more spontaneity, excitement, and joy to your lives and the lives of others.

Hollywood - Bollywood beds are more exciting!

Why do so many people get dreamy when they watch romantic stories in the movies or on television? The answer is simple. Cinema and television offer people an escape from reality and make them dream. I believe that by making people dream, the professionals of the film and television industries do their job a million times better than professionals in other sectors who dream up wars.

When we feel ourselves emotionally transported by stories we see on small or big screens, we find ourselves wishing to experience some of the transcendent magic of Hollywood in our own lives. The identification and self projection that we experience as we watch the dramatic stories of fictional characters makes us long to live out our own life stories in a more intense and meaningful way.

A negative mindset might convince you that Hollywood stories and real life are light years apart, but I would say that, at one time or another, all of us have lived Hollywood moments in which we were the protagonists and the stars of the show. There is no law written down anywhere that says we cannot live, or try to live, Hollywood moments ourselves. Without a bit of fantasy and creativity, the tables we share, and as adults, the beds we share, will not be overly exciting. As Shakespeare wisely observed long ago, "All the world's a stage and all the men and women merely players".

The entire entertainment industry constantly lures us to escape from daily preoccupations and stress, offering fictitious dream moments that we would love to make a reality. The purpose of this book is not to teach people how to live out a Hollywood romance instead of a life based on their own sensibilities and experiences. The variety of media programs out there that want to sell you celebrity lifestyles is greater than all the possible varieties of fusion food recipes previously mentioned in this book. The principles I'm proposing for adding more exciting moments to our lives do, however, have something in common with a good meal. One should be passionate in planning and preparing them and equally passionate in enjoying them. Bring your senses and your sensibilities to all you undertake. Be passionate, and above all, caring and sensitive in each and every thing you do. We will now put a special focus on the word SENSITIVE and deal with some specific situations in which our senses, our sensitivity, and our positive thinking can create the mood for more loving, exciting moments.

Your senses and your moods

How what you see affects your mood

Who would question the impact of what we see on our mood? Practically nobody! In the mood-making film and television industries, vital importance is given to the set for its ability to make the story more appealing and believable. Our daily lives are neither TV shows nor feature films (although inadvertently or purposefully we might sometimes act like they were) but focusing on the settings in which we live out our lives can make them more exciting.

There is no need at all to change all the furniture or completely redecorate a room to give it a mood-enhancing touch. A few small details can give you a new and different perception of the room and what you could be doing in it. It's a matter of figuring out what visual changes are needed to lift your mood when you are there. It helps to first make a list of all the things that are visual mood-depressors. If your bed room looks more like a prison cell or a clinical environment than a cozy nest, or if its worn-out curtains and bedclothes say more about who you were a decade ago than who you would like to be today, jot those things down on your list of things to change.

Colors have a great impact on our moods. Imagine the same room with a cool blue, fresh green, or tender pink mood makeover. The changes don't have to be permanent. Moods change! You could temporarily go all the way with a hearts and flowers motif or something even more exotic. Would your love life be improved by adding a temporary dance floor to your bedroom? **A tango with a tanga is more exciting than a slow fox trot in flannel pajamas!**

That's not to say that a very simple setting can't be just perfect. A single, well placed flower can beat the impact of the most sumptuous film set.

How what you hear affects your mood

The power of sound and music to create moods has been mentioned before in the chapter about our Affinity-mindset zones. Music probably has more power to influence our mood than any other ambient factor. It can influence what and how we perceive with our other senses. In today's digitalized world we have almost total power to control the aural elements of our environment. Our MP3 players and cellular telephones are portable mini juke boxes loaded with whatever our minds and hearts desire to hear.

The sounds of nature, our children's laughter, a dramatic crescendo in the perfect acoustic of a concert hall, or a letter from a loved one read aloud in a moment of solitude can bring us deep inner peace or arouse strong emotions.

We should always be careful to monitor the volume around us. Today's insupportably high noise levels are responsible for a plethora of physical and psychological disorders that could be cured by a little more silence around us.

If we continually surround ourselves with the cacophony of ringtones, the blasting of car horns, and the babble of the television or the CD player, they may drown out what we would most like to hear: the delicious sound of loving words whispered in our ears.

How what we smell can affect our mood

How many times has smell of the kitchen garbage can ruined your "morning candy", or the smell of naphthalene given you a headache the first few times you wore your winter coat after summer storage? We must be infinitely careful to control the unpleasant, and even toxic, odors that can invade our environment.

On the other hand, the pleasant smell of a soup simmering on the stovetop or a home-baked pie fresh from the oven comforts us, and the perfume of a garden bouquet delights us.

When the right fragrance is in the air, it puts us in the mood to sit down to eat, fall into a deep sleep, or even fall in love. Nothing is as inviting as the smell of lavender-scented sheets or as pleasurable as the smell of our favorite perfume or aftershave. People have always sought to surround themselves with pleasant aromas. It is said that Cleopatra's affinity for appealing perfumes helped her win the hearts of both Julius Caesar and Mark Antony. In Cleopatra's time, few women had access to such a luxury. Women and men of today have an almost unlimited and constantly growing array of fragrance products at their disposal. There are even colognes to make Fido smell better too!

Since the earliest of times, man has gathered aromatic plants for both cosmetic and medical purposes. Aroma therapy is an ancient healing technique that is once again being employed by professional therapists to manage pain and treat stress, anxiety, and depression. It utilizes natural essential oils that are known for their power to adjust a patient's moods as well as heal or alleviate the symptoms of a number of physical ailments.

Scientists are now exploring the ramifications of what appears to be the most subtle, but most decisive, olfactory element in sexual attraction: our pheromones. Although we use perfumes and deodorants to boost our sex appeal, according to scientists, it is the subtle and often imperceptible natural pheromones our bodies emit that send a strong and unequivocal signal to the brain of the other gender.

How what we taste affects our mood

We describe our perceptions of things that have happened to us and the characters of people around us using the terminology of taste. We often say that someone is a sweet or bitter person and we describe experiences as being delicious or relationships as having "gone sour". We use the phrase "personal tastes" to describe everything we prefer. Just a little taste of a favorite food can boost our mood incredibly. We talk about the "sweet taste of success" and even sometimes say that we long for "a little taste of excitement". That's why it is so important to treat ourselves to a morning candy and an evening sweetie every day!

How what we touch affects our mood

Our sense of touch is the first of our senses to develop while we grow in our mother's womb. Our touch receptors, that number in the millions, are distributed throughout the dermis layer of our body's skin. The skin constitutes the biggest and most sensitive organ of the human body. Its minute nerve endings detect heat, cold, pain, pleasure, and pain and serve as the data entry port for the sensations that set off the hormonal reactions that determine our moods.

Science tells us that both previous personal experiences stored in the human brain and internal and external environmental factors have important roles in how the mind interprets each new sensation sent to it by the nervous system. When a pregnant woman caresses her swollen belly, she is carrying out an act of great relevance to the future wellbeing of the child she is gestating. The warm, reassuring contact with a mother's skin during breast feeding is another gift of touch between mother and child. These are only a few examples of the many permanent impressions registered on our emotional hard disks through the sense of touch in our infancy; impressions that have important implications for our later emotional and motor development. These constitute a marvelous, natural memory affinity-mindset zone that each of us can visit to relive nurturing memories and recharge our mood battery.

The sense of touch is probably the most important sense employed in matters of human intimacy. As a consequence, it is also the most crucial sense when it comes to sharing our emotional feelings and navigating the context between our attitudes and behaviors and our perception of the attitudes and behaviors of others. We do not distinguish between physical sensations perceived through our sense our sense of touch and our emotions. We feel heat, cold, and pain but we also feel fear, joy, and pride. "Don't do that," we often say to a child. "It will hurt his feelings."

We describe something that has affected us emotionally as "a touching experience".

It is obvious that a good synchronicity between our sense of touch and our other four senses can create unlimited excitement in the most intimate spheres of our lives. It seems that the sense of touch carries more weight than the other senses in maintaining the harmony of any given situation. That in itself is exciting.

It's a fun exercise to engage all of our senses in exploring a theme. If we want life to be "just a bowl of cherries", we can search the corners of all our affinity-mindset zones and make our own sensual fantasy fusion to transform a cold and rainy Saturday into cherry blossom time. Let's give it a try.

Pull anything bright pink or red out of your closet and put it on. Make a shopping list while enjoying your morning tea or coffee. First stop: the grocery store to buy fresh cherries if they are available and won't break the bank, chocolate covered maraschino cherries for the evening sweetie, or a packet of cherry-flavored gelatin if chocolate isn't your thing or you are on a diet. Second stop: a specialty shop to pick up some naturally-scented cherry beauty products. Remember that your luxury treatments should be natural, healthy, ecologically-friendly and a fair deal for those that produce them. If a socially-conscious natural beauty products shop is on your route, go there. The Body Shop, for example, has a spectacular wild cherry line that includes Wild Cherry Body Butter, body lotion, body scrub, shower gel, lip butter, and soap made with vitamin A and E rich cherry, brazil nut, and sesame oils and Fair Trade shea butter from Africa. Third stop: a Japanese restaurant. On the way home, pass by a Japanese restaurant and order a tray of take away sushi. Before you go out the door, download Neil Diamond's "Cherry, Cherry", or one of the many fine versions of the French classic, "Le temps de cerises", if they aren't already in your music collection. With only those two downloads we already have our history, culture, and foreign language AMZs in full gear. Once back home, do a little navigating in internet. If you enter "Cherry Blossom Time Tokyo" in your browser, you will find sites that offer wonderful videos and photos of cherry trees in full bloom. Sayonara to the boredom of a dull, rainy day!

365 Valentines Days a year!

The invention of Valentine's Day was a 20th century marketing initiative to remind us that love needs to be acknowledged. It has become a world-wide expression of love, and despite the commercially- driven thinking behind it, I am not one of those who say it is an artificial campaign that has nothing to do with true feelings. It's very probable that Valentine's Day critics have an anti-celebration mindset in general and are not much given to frequent, spontaneous, reaffirmations of their most intimate relations. It is true that we shouldn't show our appreciation of those we love only when commercial interests prompt us to. It would be better to shower a little attention on those closest to us the whole year round.

We can show our affection for those close to us in a million different little ways every day instead of falling into an institutionalized once-a-year habit. A gift of a poem or candy, sending a telephone text message, making a telephone call, or doing a little job at home without the other person asking us to do it can do wonders for our relationships.

There are thousands of tiny things that can convert every day into Valentine's Day, and remembering one little detail will lead you to many other inspirations to share meaningful moments together. Little spontaneous details are much more important in building enduring relationships than occasional, excessively elaborate planned events. The less expected the gesture of appreciation, the more potential it has for generating excitement.

Our daily uniforms cover up who we really are

What most people wear every day throughout the world is determined by the climate and local social conventions. For many of us, this means putting on a literal or figurative uniform that reflects the image and values of our school, company, or social group. When we show up in the "as usual" uniform society has chosen for us, our individuality becomes muted and our mood can become muted too.

This leads us to the importance of paying attention to how what we wear affects our mood. Millions of closets, particularly women's closets, attest to how varying our daily uniform can be a mood lifter and a mood stabilizer. It's surprising how many individuals, even those with the financial means to buy fine clothing, do not take their mood into consideration when they choose what to wear. Fashion magazines and salespeople in clothing stores can help the us with hundreds of subtle but creative ideas about how to vary our wardrobe and dress better, feel more comfortable, and feel more confident.

When there is no imperative need to wear a uniform, we should wear a **Persona -form** and be more than just a head popping out of our clothing. Our body is an integral part of our personality and a vital expression of who we are. "Fine feathers make fine birds". We should preen ourselves to improve our overall perception of ourselves and the impression we make on others. Remember that choosing what to wear is a part of your morning candy.

If you are proactive in establishing a good mood when you face the morning mirror, you'll enjoy continued good feelings throughout the day. You can dress for vitality, making sure that what you put on in the morning is a positive step in beating the same old routine. Socialite Paris Hilton offers a formula to pep up one's image through fashion. As she explains, *"The only rule is, don't be boring and dress cute wherever you go. Life is too short to be blend in."* Think what you will about Paris Hilton, the young lady is never bored. She knows that fashion is a mindset and she is an expert at standing out in any setting. She's completely right about one thing: Life is too short to blend in with the crowd. An affinity for dressing well with a personal touch can liberate your spirit from a mentality of uniformity.

Going Out is coming back!

"Home sweet home" is a sincere description of our refuge from the world, a place whose sweetness grows every minute that we are away from it. Much like what you experience when you return to your own country after a trip abroad, coming back home from a day at school or the office is returning to a safe, protected haven with new insights into the world around you.

A regular escape from the daily nest adds variety to our lives, distracts us from our personal problems, and breaks the boredom of our routines. Going out is largely a matter of correctly managing both our time and our attitudes. So often time flies by without our having done anything particularly notable. Time management is as important in our leisure time as it is at work in ensuring that we do everything we should do, and a few of the things we really want to do, in the space of a day. Efficiently managing our private time is important in achieving a balance between our inner needs and the tug and pull of the world outside. As we have previously discussed, time can be regarded as money, but above all, time should be a currency we invest in improving our quality of life. Going out can double or triple the quality of those few hours we spend away from home.

A short but intense break from the routine of home can seem much longer than it really is. It's a matter of perception. Time well spent offers more than the minutes that have ticked by on the clock. As the roman dictum reminds us: *tempus fugit* (time flies). We cannot stop time, but we can make more out of it. Why not heed another Roman aphorism, *Carpe diem* (Seize the day!), and the night as well, if the right moment presents itself?

There is a naysayer always lurking in our thoughts that tries to stop us from doing the things we would like to do. His name is Mr. BUT. "Yes I would like to go out," we begin, "BUT the beds are not made ,there are dirty dishes in the sink, the ironing must be done ,the lawn should be mown, there are emails I haven't answered yet, I haven't given the kids their bath yet," etc. There will always be hundreds of things waiting to be done. The only thing that ever really gets accomplished in the 24 hours of a day is living it, which brings us back to the ever-present quality of life question.

We had better set priorities, and in the daily battle of the "Duties and Beauties" (a concept we will deal with more intensively later), give the Beauties a fighting chance. To strike a balance between the beauties and the duties, we need to learn to say WHY NOT more often, instead of automatically saying BUT. WHY NOT? It's a great idea. Let's go!!

There is an unlimited scope of possibilities to go out, adaptable to any mood and every budget. It could be taking a favorite AMZ mind escape and making it a reality. Any affinity, hobby, or special interest could inspire a short escape from your home sweet home. A sporting event, a meal in a restaurant or a picnic in the country, a concert or a movie, a night out dancing are only a few ideas. Alone, as a couple, with the entire family, or as a group of friends, these activities make great escapes from the routine. If we set our priorities with a positive, open, and active mind, we could engineer some kind of small escape from the boring routine almost every day of our lives. As we stated when we started out, the best part of going out is coming back. Coming back invigorated and refreshed will make our homes seem sweeter than ever and help us to overcome the negative things that are always a part of the reality of life.

The passion and excitement of live events

Although we have already mentioned sporting and musical events as great escapes, they deserve special attention for offering excitement at a collective level. Enthusiasm, joy, and excitement are infectious and sharing them collectively can be a spectacular mind mood event in which one feels a part of a larger community.

Sports stadiums and large concert halls bring out our ancient tribal instincts. The sense of togetherness and belonging can be very intense during a sports match or a big rock concert. There is nothing wrong with the passions they arouse as long as they are expressed in a civilized manner. Such events stimulate shared feelings at the collective level and can generate in a single night positive bonds between very diverse groups of people that would take years to develop through political sermonizing and social planning. That's powerful energy against routine and boredom on a major scale.

Five Senses and four Seasons make for unlimited excitement!

Our senses revel in the changing seasons. They were created to be the ultimate nature guides. As the seasons change, our moods change in tandem with them. The rebirth of the world around us in springtime affects us as much as it affects the birds and flowers. It is a time of renovation, dedicated to love stories, nest building, and spring house cleaning. Summer is the season of open windows, laughter on terraces, and long walks along the beach. Autumn is harvest time, the moment we enjoy what has been blessed by the sun and rain of the previous seasons. In the cold of winter, the coziness of our houses gathers us in to reflect on the passing year and make plans for the new one approaching. Each season offers us unique moments to experience the great drama of the planet's natural cycles. Each is an open invitation to our senses to observe and admire the eternal, ongoing, process of renovation, rest, and rebirth of which we are vital part. The more we live in harmony with the seasons, the more we fill our inner selves with the natural, energizing, vitality of the world.

Here are a couple of basics to help bring the seasons into our lives.

Use flower power to brighten your home. With a bit of creativity we can create amazing personalized bouquets that will bring the essence of each season into our homes and our hearts. Although florists and many super markets stock a wide variety of greenhouse plants and flowers, the best and most gratifying way to be in touch with nature is to decorate our homes with locally-grown seasonal plants and flowers. Respect all conservation laws and use common sense when gathering flowers and plants in public parks and nature reserves. Nature is a common heritage it and we must protect it.

Savor the season in your daily menus and recipes with the special tastes of each season. Think about the CO_2 emissions involved in your food purchases. Occasional purchases of exotic fruits and vegetables are certainly a treat, but the cargo planes that bring us those out-out-season delights may end up changing our local climates over time. Buying locally supports your local economy and helps preserve regional varieties of fruits and vegetables under siege by mass production elsewhere. Our children no longer know what the local season is for many of the foods they eat. Buying more seasonal fruits and vegetables helps them to learn more about the Earth's natural cycles. An excursion to a seasonal, open-air market is a nice seasonal escape from the "as usual" trip to the supermarket. Always remember that food nourishes all our senses, not just our sense of taste. A shiny apple is a delight for all the senses, from its bright, appealing color to the musical crunch it makes when we bite into it.

The colors, fragrances, tastes, and textures of the changing seasons are complemented by each season's special sounds. If you have one recording of classical music in your home, it should be Vivaldi's Four Seasons. It will inspire you to search for the composer's inspiration in nature: the sounds of birds in the countryside, the drama of a summer storm or the babbling of a brook. Don't forget the world's great heritage of seasonal music. It can be part of the soundtrack of your holiday celebrations and is a fine way of reliving seasons gone by.

A never-ending desire to learn makes for exciting daily lessons

A positive, open, and active mind is a mind that never stops learning. The Chinese proverb "Learning is a treasure that will follow its owner everywhere" is a universal truth. From the day we are born until the day we die we never stop learning, but the depth and quality of what we learn very much depends on our own attitude and the possibilities we are given. American businessman Henry L. Doherty once said a wonderful thing about the importance of learning throughout one's life:

> **"Get over the idea that only children should spend their time in study. Be a student so long as you still have something to learn, and this will mean all your life."**

The legendary Henry Ford said the same thing in a different way:

> **"Anyone who stops learning is old, whether at twenty or eighty."**

A lust for learning is the only addiction that doesn't seem to have any negative effects, as long as one's curiosity and hunger for knowledge does not lead to neglecting or forgetting the important people in one's life. We enjoy the time and effort we dedicate to learning when we feel that it makes our life more interesting and exciting.

Education was once the private preserve of the privileged. Fortunately, in today's multimedia world the door to the world of knowledge is open to many more people. Learning just one new thing that interests us every day could have an exponential impact on our lives. One exciting little lesson a day quickly adds up to 365 mind-enriching experiences a year. If we multiply that number by the years we may live, we can begin to understand what it means to live fully and well.

Excitement experienced in childhood means life-long excitement

A child without the opportunity to play would be a poor creature without fantasy, dreams, or happiness. A child is positive by nature. He starts out in life with an open mind, unburdened by prejudices, and has an infinite curiosity about the world around him. A child learns with an astounding rapidity. The more a child is exposed to new things, the more he will learn. The world of a happy child is full of games and make-believe, explorations that yield up exciting new daily discoveries.

In our advanced multimedia society, a child is grows up in a virtual world with almost no frontiers. We might think that thanks to this abundance of media, our children do not suffer from relentless routines and boredom. Unfortunately, this is not always the case. Having easy access to an amazing virtual world does not necessarily imply being well connected to the reassuring visceral protection of a home base. Without adult care and guidance, the open, unlimited world can be a lonely and confounding place devoid of a centre and too one-dimensional in terms of content. The world is a global village, but the real nucleus of that village must be a child's home.

Most kids love digital games and hundreds of millions of kids dedicate hours each day to their favorites. An absolute prohibition of digital games is not the answer to the problems that they can provoke. The mental speed, digital prowess, and imagination they teach prepare children to live in the reality of the 21st century world. This will be a century shaped by new means of audio visual communications whose technological innovations will enter our children's lives at an ever increasing speed. Our 21st century kids belong to this new world and must to grow up in synchronicity with it.

However, children have a timeless need for another form of communication, a need that is perhaps more imperative now than at any other time in human history: communication at the most intimate human level within their own homes and with their own communities. Personal warmth, care, and protection cannot be substituted by distant, virtual heroes and digital fantasy worlds. Direct human involvement, not bytes of digital information, is the best form for communicating love and understanding. Our emotional hard disk is our HEART DISK, and the happy and exciting childhood memories stored there will determine our happiness and enthusiasm for life as an adult.

The give and take of moments shared with family and community, particularly in play-time activities, teaches a child the reality of winning and losing and negotiating with others. This emotional intelligence will help him deal with his positive and negative emotions as an individual and give him the necessary skills to handle both good and bad moments in collective situations.

A child who plays will have a more exciting adulthood

To a certain extent, life is a game of winning and losing. The never ending cycle of winning and losing is part of what makes life so attractive. We never lose our childhood fascination for games. There are games for people at every stage of life. Throughout our lifetime we move from nursery toys to games played in the schoolyard and then on to sports, card games, computer games, and game shows on TV. Games can be an exciting activity and a perfect remedy against routine and boredom.

Playing as a child, one learns how to contribute wholeheartedly to team victories and to gracefully accept defeat when it is necessary. The playground is a child's training ground for the challenges he will face and the partnerships he will forge later on in life.

A well-travelled child is an inspired child

The earlier a child starts discovering the world around him, the sooner he discovers the great variety of exciting opportunities it offers him. The positive and open mind of a child that is not yet overly socialized undertakes its own tremendous learning process in a fever of excitement for all that is new and waiting to be explored. From his first day of life, a child is a natural traveler. He begins by exploring the surfaces of everything without prejudice or fear. He starts crawling, but soon begins to walk. Once walking, he begins to run, establishing new borders of known territory every day.

If we didn't stop them, our children would all go on to be world travelers like Marco Polo or Ibn Batutta, forever seeking new horizons. Unfortunately, crossing borders implies facing dangers they have yet to learn about and we cannot let them explore without our guidance and protection. For the open mind of a youngster, the worst dangers of all can be the artificial borders created by parents who have grown up in a socially and philosophically limited world and seek to protect their children from all other values and realities. These parents are products of closed societies that cultivate a sense of their own superiority and a fear of outside influences. The unfounded, ignorant belief that they are superior to others is a poisonous legacy they pass to the next generation.

Fortunately, most 21st century parents and teachers are more open-minded and recognize the importance of widening children's horizons. They recognize the value of travel in a child's development and know that a single trip to a completely new place can add more to a child's knowledge and good judgment than a hundred narrow-minded lessons at home.

A well-travelled child is an inspired child and will automatically have a more stimulating and exciting life as an adult. Just as learning is a treasure that will follow its owner everywhere, early travel experiences constitute a life-long compendium of useful references for coping with and making the most out of any new situation one encounters later in life.

A loved child is a loving adult

Our capacity to love others depends strongly upon how much love we ourselves received in our childhood. This is a much more important factor than socio-economic background in determining our ability to properly nurture another generation. The most important thing we inherit from our family should be our emotional and spiritual heritage, but that is not a given on any rung of the socio-economic ladder. The basic right to parental love may be written on the Magna Carta of our hearts, but not all of us have had the luck to have learned the art and skills of loving from our parents. Pierre Teilhard De Chardin wrote that "Love is the affinity which links and draws together the elements of the world". He called it, "the agent of universal synthesis". Unfortunately, a person who has never learned to love will not enjoy life in the same way that others do, and will have less successful relationships and fewer opportunities to share happy and exciting moments.

A person blessed with a deep capacity for loving also tends to be more positive, open-minded, open- handed, and open-hearted. He is naturally more inspired to create exceptional moments and has less risk of falling into boring routines. The positive and negative energy we inherit affect the way we approach life and how much we enjoy it. If we have been fortunate enough to have been well-loved and cared for in our childhood, we are in a better position to perpetuate the cycle of positive energy that we were born into. We should share our inherited positive energy with others and use it constantly to buoy up our own moods.

A thesis on the excitement of learning
is a lesson we will never forget

Our years of formal education form a bridge between our childhood dependency upon others and our adult independence and responsibility toward the community and the society we live in. A child's initiation in the academic world can be marked by his critical attitude toward "the system" and the new responsibilities and tasks it requires of him. There are good reasons for this.

Not all educational institutions are great examples of how instill enthusiasm for personal and civic responsibility in young people. Young people's rebellion against the system should be regarded as a healthy generational check-up that signals society of the need to move more in one or direction or another.

The famous French refrain *Liberté, fraternité, eqalité!* (freedom, brotherhood, equality) that revolutionized 18th century French society is still regularly repeated on university campuses round the world, wherever free speech and dissidence are permitted. As long as upcoming generations show a vivid interest for the future, they are going to take a critical look at the norms of the societies they live in and call for changes in its system of values and standards. Most young people are idealistic. They seek to create a better world and desire to put their energy into something constructive that will result in a better and more just future for all. As long as new generations of young people continue to place their hope in a better world and dedicate their will to correcting existing inequalities, the dream of a human utopia will edge its way slowly toward reality. If younger generations lacked the innate drive to question the past, where would we find the energy to contemplate needed change? By their nature, established systems with their rigid rules resist change. Even the most vanguard institutions quickly succumb to the temptation of rejecting change in favor of promoting their own continuity.

While it's fascinating to analyze the challenges that entering an academic environment presents to young people, it's more important to reflect on how students could get more out of their academic years, really enjoy the excitement of learning, and learn as individuals how to bring about constructive and inspiring change in their own lives and the world around them. Any change that is made in the world begins with the mental capacity of an individual to imagine it. The roots of change are in a person's mindset. A student with a positive, open, and active mind should be able to develop himself as a human being while he strives for academic excellence.

As a part of every program of study, universities and schools should offer a course on mental fitness designed to help young people learn how to balance their future quality of life with the expectations the world will have for them once they graduate. I'm not talking about exhorting them to work hard and to seek excellence, but explaining to them the cold reality that often lies behind all that hard work and top performance. After graduation, hard work and excellence are often equated by society with placing a higher value on competitiveness than on team work, working day and night to meet unreasonable performance targets, and selling one's soul in a never-ending struggle for power and money. The better the student, the more easily he or she can become imprisoned in a rat race that has nothing to do with the excellence and ethics preached in the halls of learning.

Students should be taught how established personal habits and "as usual" routines contribute to their sense of boredom, drain their energy and lead to de-motivation. If a young person never learns how to properly use a study period, for example, he may never be able to organize himself to learn new things on his own once liberated from a structured academic environment. It is important to deal with such issues as self-organization, concentration, and motivation while the child still has a flexible attitude and a naturally inquiring mind.

One's student years should be the time to begin writing a personal thesis about how to challenge social conventions and achieve a balance between one's personal dreams and his social obligations. Studying this subject would provide the ambitious and inspired student with a personal roadmap that indicated a way out of the seeming contradictions between high social and economic achievement and a personal life full of satisfying and exciting moments.

 A student with a positive, open, and active mind trained to manage his time well and establish relevant priorities might title his thesis "Time spent studying something exciting is never lost time". It would be a thesis he would edit over and over again his whole life through, continually adding new and exciting ideas.

Exciting work produces rewarding results

If you don't like your work you will never be productive on the job. If we don't like what we have to do to pay the bills, we can never expect to give a great performance; and if we don't perform on the job, both our professional and private lives will suffer. A disastrous private life can also lower our performance at work, even if we love our job. Our professional and private lives are inextricably linked, whether we like it or not.

For almost all of us, our working hours represent the longest part of our day. It is vital to have sufficient positive exciting moments during this time in order to keep ourselves inspired, motivated, and in a good state of mind.

We would all like to have the opportunity to throw ourselves enthusiastically into a job that would benefit ourselves, our colleagues, and the company or institution we work for. These so-called "win-win" jobs allow everyone to maintain a high performance level without falling victim to professional burn-out. Achieving exceptionally good results makes a job exciting and having an exciting job makes achieving exceptional results easier. Stifling "as usual" work environments with their routine and boredom have no place in advanced societies seeking to keep up with the rhythm of 21st century progress.

 Most of the topics dealt with in previous chapters are totally applicable to the work place. When it comes to relatively routine jobs, the need to alleviate work-related stress and burn-out through physical and mental escapes cannot be overstated. In cases in which one's job demands a high level of creativity and mental effort, the concept of the triple mind alliance is a very useful tool. The key to achieving innovation is having a positive, open, and active mind.

Professional incest leads to mental miscarriages!

 A certain level of routine is necessary in some jobs for motives of efficacy, but in dynamic and innovation driven business environments, routine is counterproductive and in extreme cases may even lead to the failure of the company. For jobs that require high levels of repetitive actions, within the near future job bank descriptions of the position may best coincide with a mechanical or cyber robot's professional profile. I'm not kidding, and I'll give you two reasons why robots will be the better candidates for the job: First, they are always happy as long as someone occasionally greases their moving parts or plugs them in when the workday begins, and secondly, they will make few mistakes and will never go on strike, ask for a paid vacation, or file a complaint with the labor board. For jobs that require human labor, routine is the nemesis of inspiration and progress. The common obsession for sticking with the out-dated, solutions, the famous "yes but" resistance to innovation and change, and relentless routines demoralize employees and constitute a slow cancer that destroys a company's competitive edge.

Other assassins of inspiration and exciting new opportunities are technocrats and bureaucrats. Everything they conceive, even after a long and expensive gestation period, ends in a total mental miscarriage. Professional incest can cause the degeneration of complete departments or companies while the culprits gleefully celebrate record numbers of endless power point presentations full of everything save POWER and a POINT. Routine based on complex systems and iron guidelines are the friends of the ordinary, and these working environments are characterized by an excess of inefficient stress and deficit of efficient excitement.

Exciting ideas get born in healthy chaos!

Creativity and inspiration need a positive working environment in which respect, freedom of expression, and motivation replace an inflexible authority that offers more rules and regulations than inspirational guidance. Exciting ideas are born in an environment where an individual's initiative has a higher value than his ability to be a resigned workaholic and a mindless producer of tons of useless reports. A round-the-clock subordinate who has never innovated or added value to a project outcome is headed for professional burnout. Creativity and inspiration reign where healthy, balanced minds work in a healthy, exciting, and moderately chaotic environment free of strangling routines.

Mindful meditations are better than brainstorming!

For many years, so-called brain storming sessions have been touted as the best means to create exciting new ideas and open up new business opportunities. While proof certainly exists that good results can often come out of this collective procedure, it is interesting to note that most of the great innovations that have changed society have not come out of committees or brainstorming sessions, but were the inspirations of individual great minds and entrepreneurs who worked alone. It's more than possible that having no committee or multi-level authority to judge their nascent ideas and stifle them with a constant negative shower of BUTS was a factor in their making their visions concrete realities. The brain can be stormed, but throughout history the greatest thinkers and artists have not created their most exciting ideas or works in a state of mental turbulence, but through mindful meditation. Thinking through a problem or turning an idea over and over in one's head until the right answer comes is the formula for all great accomplishments.

Time spent thinking is more exciting than time spent doing!

Having limited time to accomplish a large number of assigned tasks provokes intense stress. When this situation occurs, either too many tasks have been assigned to one person or the person has a serious time management problem. I personally believe the latter is the greater factor in provoking stress and I am convinced that **a lot more priority should be given to time spent thinking than to time spent doing**. Time management is more an attitude than a system or procedure. This isn't a new idea at all. Michael Kastner, a German psychologist and professor, expressed his opinion of time management in 1946, saying: "Time management is nonsense. You cannot manage time but only change your attitude."

Mr. Kastener's quote should not be taken in any absolute sense, but in relative terms, it confirms that without a consciousness of time and a will to master the basics of organization, setting priorities and maintaining schedules will not be easy. Parallel to what I have said in previous chapters about time being money but quality time being invaluable, I believe that

spending more time thinking trumps doing things without having thought them through sufficiently.

Business is not an exception. Taking time to think creates added value down the line, increases production quality, and ensures better results. When efficient time management means having the time to manage efficiently, it is a major contributor to positive outcomes and better working environments.

Leadership is Sensor-ship and more exciting!

Leaders must maintain open channels of communication with the people they are leading. It is crucial that a superior transmits his acquired knowledge and skills to subordinates. What makes a really great leader is his emotional intelligence and capacity to understand other people and his grasp of the essentials in constantly fluctuating situations. Self-knowledge is a precondition for leading others. True leaders have learned to manage their own ups and downs and remain steady and balanced in challenging moments. Understanding what makes others tick and showing sensitivity toward all team members are key requirements for leadership in any field.

Leaders have keen senses and are good listeners and observers who can size up a person or situation in seconds. Leadership is Sensor-ship: a sense of humanity, business sense and common sense.

The hidden artist in all of us

In the chapter "Awakening and supercharging our senses" we talked about learning from artists and craftsmen. To create something is an exciting, very personal, and extremely gratifying experience. The open minds and heightened senses of creative people open the door of inspiration and creativity to them. The words routine and boredom are not a part of their vocabulary. The good news is that all people have some artistic corner deep inside them. There are many unknown artists hidden among us; people that just naturally have a good feeling for expressing ideas and emotions visually or through music. Travelling around the world, I have been impressed by the artistic skills of the simplest people living in the most remote places.

Having a creative hobby makes hundreds of millions of people around the world feel more alive and more connected to the universe they live in. Creative activity is a stimulus for all the senses and is a more conscious way of experiencing and enjoying the world around us. Everyone should try to develop their natural skills and explore their creative affinities, even if it is just for the sake of having a creative outlet to share with others.

Making the most of our mature years: Excitement first! Health second!

This title might seem at first glance a bit unrealistic. Good health is essential at any point in our in lives and the more we mature, the more we appreciate it. Health really should be our number one priority, but I just wanted to call attention to the crucial contribution our attitude makes in keeping us young. A youthful and vigorous mindset can help slow down the aging process and make us feel more vital and alive. During our mature years, routine and boredom can easily put us in a mental rut if we don't actively seek out new and exciting daily experiences. In my opinion, the very best recipe for staying healthy longer is to be a vital part of society as long as we can. For many retired people who don't utilize their new free time well, a pension is a form of poison. Retirement, which offers the opportunity to do so many invigorating things, makes un-motivated people feel more tired than when they were working all day long. If the body and mind are in good condition, prolonged activity, rather than an advanced retirement, is the best remedy against premature aging.

Unfortunately, our society tends to put excellent, experienced employees out to pasture just at the moment that they could add most value to the company, arguing that replacing them with the new brains and bodies is the best way to maintain performance levels. This misguided policy often puts young, inexperienced professionals driven by short term interests in control of operations that require experience and a steady hand. The one-dimensional management practices these newcomers tend to utilize are frequently the root of many corporate problems. The best balance of youthful vigor and proven experience is usually found in companies where various generations work together and there is a constant interchange of fresh new ideas and knowledge acquired over time. Good examples are multi-generational family companies where a respect for different generational viewpoints gives the business a sense of continuity and stability.

Yesterday's memories are today's excitement and tomorrow's dreams

It is a known fact that as we progressively age, we tend to forget things that happened yesterday but remember with astounding clarity the things that happened many years ago, particularly details of our childhood.

This means that we should make the best of every moment of the present. Now is the moment to record many interesting, exciting moments on our HEART DISKS, in order to relive them with great pleasure in the future. Today's hobbies, sports activities, creative exercises, study programs, mental or physical travelling, and encounters with loved ones and friends are the stuff of tomorrow's dreams.

One cannot make up for a long, boring life trying to pack in a lifetime's worth of excitement in old age. Enthusiasm, curiosity, and joy of living can atrophy if not exercised continually from childhood on. Maintaining a positive mindset is life's greatest achievement. It opens doors to unexpected and wonderful experiences, wherever we are and whatever we do. Looking back on a life well lived, instead of regretting a life of lost opportunities, is the coronation of our brief existence on this planet.

The daily challenge of balancing the "Beauties" and "Duties" of life

I have suggested so many ways to beat the routine and turn boredom into excitement that you may now be thinking that it's easier said than done. I admit that it's easier to talk about things than to make them happen, but this is no reason not to take up the challenge. Many great things can be realized through small changes in our attitude and consciousness.

Every little initiative that contributes to our greater happiness is an important step forward, and if we can establish a positive mindset, we have already won half the battle. The other half of winning the war against routine and boredom is managing our time and our attitude. We must defend our real priorities and that depends upon carrying out our duties efficiently in order to have time for the beauties of life. Has it ever occurred to you that almost everything we do could wait, or be done by somebody else? No one is irreplaceable in absolute terms. This becomes completely clear to you in those moments when bad luck or fate intervenes and prevents you from doing the tasks that before seemed inevitably and invariably to be your responsibility alone.

Although many of the things we routinely do must be done, some are less relevant than others. We should put some forethought into these routine duties to ensure that we are not just mechanically doing non-essential things that are robbing us of precious time for the far more essential beautiful things of life. Taking time out for the beauties of life will give us energy to improve the quality of our duty work.

PART III: KEEP THE MIND EXCITED!

Wing to Wing travelling shortens distances and deepens memories

Whether and how we travel are personal decisions. What we get out of travel greatly depends upon our attitude. Our positive, open, and active mind will guide us in planning our mental and physical itineraries, influence our mood on the road, and determine how much we enjoy our trip.

Even when we indulge in a little mind travel, we might want to share our thoughts about the trip with someone we feel good about. A post mind travel discussion with a good friend is a great way to keep in touch and can be a mechanism for navigating together through the endless universe of reflections and feelings.

Travelling with other people who share our affinities makes a trip more exciting. Being in good company reduces our perceived travel time on long trajectories and sharing exciting moments deepens our memory of a journey. Travelling together is travelling wing to wing and sharing heart to heart the experience of a great escape. Memories are the best souvenir of our travels.

Moments spent remembering are also great moments

We naturally give priority to consciously enjoying the everyday moments we live, especially in periods of great personal momentum. Living the present intensely is creating a great reservoir of memories that are decisive in dealing with what the future brings. The overall feeling of happiness for having enjoyed life, having committed ourselves to challenging tasks, and having achieved goals will be there for us to draw on in less stimulating moments. Facing difficult times with few good memories to reflect upon is an unenviable situation for anyone. It's comparable to trying to fight off a disease with a depressed immune system. It's important to be aware of the good things that have happened to us in the past and be grateful for them. This doesn't imply living exclusively in the past and not focusing sufficiently on the present and future. We can nurture the present and the future with inspiring personal and collective memories without falling into permanent state of nostalgia.

National holidays and commemorations of great world events can inspire our future actions. Think of the inspiration that Americans draw from 4th of July celebrations that mark their Declaration of Independence and the feelings of pride that the French feel remembering the storming of the Bastille on the 14th of July 1789. How many emotions are stirred in Germany on the 3rd of October when thousands of people come together to celebrate Unification Day and commemorate the fall of the Berlin wall!

What would be our lives be like if we never celebrated our birthdays, the birth of our children, or the golden wedding anniversaries of our parents and grandparents? Ceremonies that mark our entry into our respective communities such as first communions and bar mitzvahs, or our achievements, such as graduations, sports championships, or academic prizes become important memories. In Japan, the second Monday in January is a national holiday that celebrates the coming of age of everyone who will celebrate their twentieth birthday that year.

Good memories are a launch pad for our future aspirations. Our memory is a reservoir that feeds our moods with both positive and negative recollections of the past. The more priority we give to reliving the good moments, the more positive our overall perception of our lives will be.

We can extend our enjoyment of pleasant experiences by giving them what I call the triple attention treatment. The triple attention treatment is not only enjoying a specific event when it happens, but also fully savoring the thrill of the expectations we feel before and the memories of the event that come after. If we fully enjoy the Pre-During-Post experience, we will triple our good memories of any happy event. Our memories of a special trip should always include the excitement of the anticipation as well as the pleasure of the time actually spent travelling. The joy of preparing for a long-anticipated journey cannot be overestimated. Reading about the destination, preparing all the things we will need to take, making the reservations, etc., is really its own exciting adventure. Sharing travel memories with friends and family always gives us great pleasure, and mentally revisiting all the phases of a special journey in a quiet moment alone can give us a deep sense of satisfaction. The more we fill up our memory reservoirs with triple impact memories, the more rewarding it will be to remember.

Excitement you have lived is a nice give away

When we travel we often buy souvenirs for our friends and relations as a way of letting them know that we thought about them during the trip and of sharing some of the exciting moments of the voyage. In many cases, the best souvenir is sharing our impressions face to face when we return. A conversation about our trip might be a needed breath of fresh air for another person who hasn't been able to get away recently. People like to hear and to learn from others' life experiences. Your timely sharing of a happy trip may be the best travel give away on earth and a perfect way to break the routine and boredom of stale "as usual" conversations with friends and family.

Many television stations have popular programs based on sharing experiences and don't forget those internet blogs and chat rooms designed to interchange travel experiences. Your commentaries may help create better Pre-During-Post travel experiences for others.

Keep your wings spread!

You don't get a pilot's license after only a couple of flights. We should practice our take off and landing skills frequently. As I stated earlier, happiness is not a destination but a way of living. Every day of our lives should be a unique destination and an opportunity for spreading our wings.

Even if it sometimes seems difficult, never stop striving to put more excitement in your life and never stop dreaming about what you really want to do. If you nurture your determination with vitamins of hope, even when the facts seem to be against you, it will give you a tremendous power to achieve things. I've always liked the following anonymous quotation:

> **"Never give up on what you really want to do. The person with big dreams is more powerful than one with all the facts."**

Let's recap a few of the main points that can help you establish an anti-routine and anti-boredom mindset:

- **A positive mind is the entrance door to good feelings.**
- **An open mind nurtures an active mind.**
- **An active mind is never bored.**
- **An active mind is rewarded by many creative inspirations.**
- **We should live every moment intensely and consciously.**
- **Time is money but, more importantly, time is life.**
- **Our minds have wings. We can travel mentally as well as physically.**
- **Transforming "as usual" boredom into excitement depends upon our daily attitude.**
- **We must keep our wings spread to be fit for our next great life adventure.**
- **Enjoy exceptional and exciting moments every day.**

The many tips I give in this book are only a starting point for discovering many wonderful new ways of getting more joy out of living. If this book might have inspired you to focus more on beating your own personal routine and boredom, I will consider the time I dedicated to writing it time well spent. By developing a positive, open, and active mind and applying some of the ideas given in this book, you will have created a good base for living a more exciting and fulfilling life. Starting out is half the journey.

It's worth remembering that we only live once. Time may be money but our top priorities should be a healthy body, a peaceful soul, and a happy mind. The big events aren't what will make our lives truly great and satisfactory. The hundreds of thousands of little "unusual" exciting moments etched on our hard and heart disks will be what determine the mood registered every morning on our life mirror.

 Whether life is worth living will strongly depend upon what we make out of it. The philosopher Bertrand Russell, one of the greatest thinkers of the 20th century, had a critical view of human behavior and spent a lifetime studying how the positive and negative aspects of society affected the lives of individuals. In the preface to his autobiography, *What I Have Lived For*, written at the age of 84, Russell stated that three passions had governed his life: "the longing for love, the search for knowledge, and unbearable pity for the suffering of mankind." He acknowledged that "love and knowledge, so far as they were possible, have led me upward toward the heavens. But always pity brought me back to earth," adding: "Pain makes a mockery of what human life should be. I long to alleviate the evil, but I cannot, and I too suffer. This has been my life. **I have found it worth living, and would gladly live it again if the chance were offered me.**"

In spite of this great man's critical attitude toward the world and his own life, in the end he made an overall positive assessment about what he made out of it. Life can be hard. No one will refute this. Routine and boredom can definitely contribute to its hardness. Bertrand Russell made it a personal philosophy not to give the latter a chance and trusted in love, knowledge and empathy for others to make his life meaningful. This is the clear message he left to us, as so many other positive, open, and active minds did before and after him.

Let's keep our wings spread!

Final Acknowledgements

I would like to extend my sincere thanks to all the readers of this book for the reflections they make and actions they take during and after reading it.

I can't tell you how gratifying it is for me that readers who have experienced for themselves how a positive, open, and active mind can help beat routine and boredom, share my methods with colleagues, friends, and loved ones. It implies an exponential multiplication of the number of people getting more joy out of life and living exciting moments.

As has been stated various times throughout this book, every single exciting moment is a valuable contribution to living better and loving life more. How wonderful it is to be alive!!! The following little poem is dedicated to the readers of this book and to every person who loves living or wants to get more out of life. There are millions of marvelous feelings and inspirations that can be derived from our relationships with other people and from the natural world around us. If we study human nature, and nature itself, the beauty and diversity of their divine creation will never cease to surprise and delight us. May your conviction that it's worth beating the routine and boredom lead you to enjoy many exciting and exceptional moments. Life is worth living and each one of us deserves to experience it to the maximum!

"Living is loving life"
Live to love life.
Live to love its diversity and beauty
Love chance and live duty.
Love from the heart, the vital drive.
Love the people-nature bound
Live the divine creation
Live the rewarding fascination,
The truth that, "Loving life is living!"
That will confirm its ground
And become a daily sensation.
Theo Kerstjens
(20-08-09)

www.ingramcontent.com/pod-product-compliance
Lightning Source LLC
Chambersburg PA
CBHW051426280526
45785CB00003B/1179